Island of
Lightning

*For Decima
and for Ffion*

Robert Minhinnick

Island of Lightning

SEREN

Seren is the book imprint of
Poetry Wales Press Ltd
Nolton Street, Bridgend, Wales

www.serenbooks.com
facebook.com/SerenBooks
Twitter: @SerenBooks

ISBN 978-1-78172-129-2
Mobi 978-1-78172-172-8 (mobi)
Epub 978-1-85411-173-5 (epub)

A CIP record for this title is available from the British Library

The publisher works with the financial assistance
of the Welsh Books Council

Printed by the CPI Group (UK) Ltd., Croydon

Contents

Yellow Mountain Fever

1. Nine Dragons Peak

I have a world apart, wrote Du Fu, that is not amongst men.

The lines reoccur as I wait my turn. My turn to move. To return to low ground. Because my heart is not in the highlands. I'm a sea-level sort. But there are thousands of us here. Up here. In the Huangshan mountains. Thousands eating cucumber-flavoured crisps. Thousands of us on the last weekend of the season and on these helter skelter paths there's a crush tighter than the Shanghai metro. Up here on the ledge. But worse. Worse because we're high. Much too high.

To my right is the cliff. A panic attack's geology. Despite its banded porphories, it's a mind-whitening abyss. How easy to vanish. Like a meteor scratch. I imagine my own trajectory, the gorge rising to meet me.

But there's no chance of slipping. Asphyxiation's more likely. Surrounded by tourists I peep around at this world heritage site. And feel a paean in the neck coming on.

2. Echo Wall

Mao Zedong wrote poems, killed poets. He feared the revolutions in their heads. Mao also hated tigers. They did not fit in. Now the first tiger seen in China for thirty years stalks the internet. There it is in silhouette – China's grave soul revealed. Out of its own history the tiger steps, feet like chrysanthemums. Out of the earth its aphrodisiac bones.

3. Immortal Drying the Boot

I gave the talk in a pagoda in the village. Afterwards in the WC, a pig pushed its snout through the wall.

Never turn your back on a sow, I remembered a voice from childhood. But this pig was a goddess, bristles like fishbones, hogskin pale as curd.

Later at the banquet, pigs' ears were served, cut into strips. They looked and tasted like elastic bands. Never trust a poet, young porkers might be told. Especially vegetarian ones.

4. Cloud Dispelling Mansion

Still here. On the mountain's hard shoulder. We're still here. Under my foot a butterfly decayed like a text message, the people around me sharing sunflower seeds.

They seem cheerful enough. Obviously they're used to congestion. To cope, I adopt a dream strategy. A week earlier I had stood in my sunflower grove. It was dusk and the church of St John the Baptist squat as a fort. The base camp of a military god. Soon it would be time to cut the sunflowers. To burn that green meat. I could picture their pendulums and bamboo trunks.

No, I decided. If I wait to fell them and instead study their metamorphosis, the sunflowers will become rusted bicycles. And afterwards wreathwire, roadsigns, scrap iron scions. Give them another week in the Baptist's plot. Because they still loomed tall as traffic lights. Each sunflower face a flitch aflame.

5. Golden Turtle View of the Ocean

Spies, my companion had said. And the children of spies. And the blameless children of the children of spies. They will all be shamed. Even after they shred the documents, the spies will be revealed.

If democracy (has such a term meaning now?) comes to China, it will instigate a reckoning like no other in history.

This morning I watched archetypal peasants tend iconic water buffalo. In the medieval labyrinth of streets the chestnut peelers and copper-cutters behaved immemorially. A zither played, a little girl peed on a melon vine. In the east Shanghai's dioramas rose against an inkstone sky.

6. Mobile Phone Rock

At the temple I had asked my translator what religion she was.

I am a member of the Chinese Communist Party, she said.

So this isn't really your bread and Buddha then?

She looked away. But brightened.

Have you tasted our rice wine? she inquired.

I've heard it's dangerous, I say.

So is religion.

7. Jade Screen Peak

I wondered, what is the secret? Of sunflowers? Before I incinerate my sunflowers will I sense their souls? In the now or never as the pyre is lit, will sunflowers reveal themselves? When, at the bonfire's heart, the sunflowers are a pulse of pale opals, will their mystery be explained? But I knew the answer. The sunflowers will suffer immolation. Yet evade death. They will never be what I want them to be. After their season they bow and bleed. But even as they lie in state they are planning the next coup.

Because there is always a flaw in sunflowers. A dark leaf in the corner of a corona. Their perfection is not perfect. Betrothal and betrayal have a common root.

Under the sunflowers I listened to the crickets. All year I had waited and now they were singing. Homer, Du Fu, knew the music of those satirists in the grass. Plangent their pleading, its neurasthenic B minor. Pointless as old men's wisdoms.

8. Stage of the Fairy-Mother Goddess

Before us, the *mochyn*-machine had been disassembled. The

cuisines of Anhui province are particularly piggy. But as various cogs and pulleys of the pig resemble tofu, I stuck it out. Like planets the dishes revolved. A bowl of flames resembled veronica petals. Dark pucks of pork spun past. Again that voice from childhood reoccurred. *Brawn*, it said. *Brisket*. The chalice of the *chitterlings*. Okay, I sighed. One last time for tripe's tropes.

9. Heavenly City Peak

It's still like the Hunan highway up here. I once read that to dream of a castle means the gratification of desire. A dull dream indeed. I dream of the big house in Cwrt Colman, the hotplate of its lawns. In the fog its bone-coloured roses seem to shrink and swell. But nothing is moving, there's no pursuit. No anxiety. Then I turn the corner of my dream. There's a gravel path and a peacock with its tail spread in the dust.

To dream of swimming, they say, means bad luck. To dream of a seabird means danger. I dream of a cormorant, its beak a piton. I have come with the cormorant to graze the scurvygrass on Sker while from the sea at midnight I gaze at the screed of stars and the aeroplanes coming in and yes it's that EasyJet from Alicante with Mr Cory Evans of Fairyland, Neath, in his golden sombrero, and Mrs Kayleigh Evans with a donkey stuffed with chocolate Euros. Then I wake. I'm still on the mountain. Shuddering amidst its granite spires. The family around me are drinking sugarcane juice, passing round a persimmon.

10. Purple Cloud Peak

They say Du Fu became a poet because he failed his civil service examinations. Perhaps we should teach our children that it is dangerous to pass exams. Because failing an exam should make us think. Failing an exam means we remain in the world's wild places where complacency's poisons cannot reach. Now here, on Huangshan, a dragonfly. In the crimson of its guild.

And here, as a flat Mongolian face lights up, the *Mission Impossible* ringtone. But suddenly we are moving and after an hour we reach the cable car and then the bamboo forests are rushing towards us and the tea bushes planted amongst the bamboo pass like rain clouds. That's what I need. Seaweedy tea in a lidded cup. Everlastingly refilled.

Why don't you do something about Burma? I ask the translator on the way down.

Yes. We should nuke the generals. That might teach them.

China could help, I say.

Those monks! she hisses. The people have to feed them. The people who can't feed themselves. They're crafty as cats, those monks. Greedy as dragons. Europe woke up to lazy monks centuries ago.

The saffron revolution, I say. Maybe it's coming your way.

I look around. Somehow it's evening. Chinese characters wink like hoarfrost on the highway.

Never, she says. But smiles. And suggests we might stop at the restaurant of the laughing pig.

Hmm, I say. Pigs don't have much to laugh about round here.

Perhaps you need that drink. We call it *bei ju*.

Why not? I answer. Especially when the rest of the world is drinking cappuccino. By the way. Hasn't Starbucks opened in the Forbidden City?

Well, yes, she says. But I think you'll find that they are about to disappear. Very soon. Very soon indeed.

The Outlook from Felin Gwcw

I'm on the train.

By their nokias ye shall know them.

I put down my newspaper and look out the window. And there it is, glimpsed in a second. Or at least the place where it might be. Or where it used to be.

But there are so many trees that suddenly erupt, their lava refashioning the landscape, a landscape I should know but fail to interpret, having been otherwise occupied for a moment, a moment in which a new geology has been created and a molten world cooled.

And now it is gone or I am elsewhere, on the journey's endless elsewhere. But in that moment I determine to go back. Or really, to visit for the first time. To visit Felin Gwcw.

How does a place stop being a place? When Crewe Alexandra drew with Halifax Town a thread was cut. Immediately the joists began to warp, mortar to drift from its joints in Felin Gwcw's cool vale. A new narrative commenced.

The last people to live at Felin Gwcw did the football pools. When the eighth draw came up they knew they could escape to a world of electricity and mains water, away from the sulphurous steam with which the trains running ten feet away on the south Wales-London line drenched their home.

But Felin Gwcw was there before the railway, before professional football. It was a house and a workplace, a mill built on a field of ragged robin beside the Nant Ffornwg.

Today that fierce current is feeble after two dry months. I'm wading downstream as if I was driving the water, a water-drover urging it on towards the confluence where the Ffornwg forgoes its name and finally forgets itself.

I'm walking in the streambed because this summer afternoon it is the only way to reach Felin Gwcw. As a child here, the ferns met over my head. I walked in their world of green anthracite. Today white umbels crowd the sky. I am baptised in sap.

So I step into the river and wade with the gwrachens under the alder and the eels in the stoups and stillwaters beneath the elder and watch a heron like some Egyptian god inscribed on a Ffornwg-coloured tablet.

The stream runs beneath the mill wall, so low today that the craftsmanship of millers and masons is revealed. Few people for generations can have seen this stonework, its exactitudes under my hands felted with loaves of moss.

In my memory Felin Gwcw has always been a ruin. And known no cuckoos, only owls, owls to taunt any trespasser, but especially at twilight when the sky is the colour of an owl's egg and the owls, those amber-eyed alchemists, are transmuting moods, so that the child that was hurried in shadow with owls' feathers in his belly and owls' talons in his hair, hurried up the path that no longer exists and under the railway tunnel that does, the wagons passing overhead in a monsoon of acid smoke, blotting the light out with owls' wings, their roaring of *how-good-are-you-good-are-you* filling his head with an owlish cacophony.

These days a hazel wood surrounds Felin Gwcw. Briars like bowsaws and the white bones of ivy cover its walls. I stop short. There are people, I'm sure, conspiring; strangers, invaders, conniving.

But it is the Ffornwg's phonics I overhear, a soliloquy I should have recognised, those syllables being part of my own speech. And everywhere is hart's tongue and a starlight of stitchwort. Yet how easily my vocabulary sloughs its skins. Suddenly I am naked. Suddenly my flesh of words has disappeared. This is the dawn of time. This is a world before language. Here are stone and air and flowering things. Here is nettle dust. Here is water. Here are light's encryptions on the retina. Here is my pulse. Here is everything I knew unmade, and the silence's indictment of my fatuity.

Felin Gwcw too is unmade and yet proves irreducible. And then the train crashes past and I am looking at a man with a newspaper who for an instant is staring out at a place that does not exist and of which I have always been an inhabitant, a man who looks through me unseeing and is then amazed at how close I am, my bramble body that clings to Felin Gwcw, my dog rose eyes so near to him that he recoils as if he has glimpsed a ghost, and yes, I think, yes, he is right about that.

Are You Lonesome Tonight?

1.

Don't you know there's a hurricane coming? a man asked, pushing on into the sand.

There's always a hurricane, I said. Around here. We should be used to it.

2.

Chunky tyres, that's what this bicycle has. It's a mountain bike, a red and blue Emmelle, bought second hand, allowing me to go straight over kerbs and the speed humps on the sand-strewn, sometimes buried road across the badlands into the caravan site.

I was coming back through the fairground but cycling was hard work. Eventually I had to stop and push. Out of the west I had flown but heading home was arduous. Nothing else for it, I had to interrupt the journey and take shelter under an awning in the fairground. The wind was whipping the tide white. I could feel its sting.

The journey to the allotment goes past Dolly's Cabin and Robert's Ice Cream, straight through the fair, on through the flattened dunes and dismantled chalets, then into Trecco Bay. It takes me round one of the biggest caravan sites in Europe, down its High Street that at this time is full of holidaymakers. Only in December will the gates be padlocked and my way obstructed. Then, to save time, I have to drive or cycle a longer route.

When I finish fossiling and walk off the ridge, down from the moon-coloured corals of Cog y Brain, this is the way I come. In the limestone light the sea is blue as buckthorn. There runs its horizon, glimpsed behind the aisles of caravans and the neon signs for Coast restaurant and Costcutter. A squadron of turnstones passes over the barbecues in the sand, whilst the last ingots are cooling. Last rubies…

And every day that sand is different. In this wind it's a smoky glacier and the wind has blown every day this summer, a neurasthenic nag over the waves, sculpting the drifts and dune crests, revealing what has been lost, concealing what I might have considered permanent.

Might have. But I have lived here too long to believe anything can remain unchanged. Over a formica tabletop at the Blue Dolphin café, in my scalp after an expedition to Rhych, the sand will announce itself. Sand finer than scurf. Sand sharper than swarf.

But bravado cuts no ice in the fairground. With relief I dismount and start pushing. And that's where I see her. She is waving goodbye to a group of five other women, several in what I supposed are fifties' flared skirts and bobby sox. But looking uncertain. They pause outside the Hi Tide, the likeliest choice, but then are blown off course and decide to try The Buccaneer next door. The group turns around, the woman I'd noticed again in two minds. They are splitting up, but her bus won't be here for an hour.

The last time I visited The Buccaneer was with the poet, Iwan Llwyd. I had promised to demonstrate some 'real fairground Porthcawl', that would match The Buck's reputation.

I know who these women are. They are the advance party for the Elvis Festival, now annual in Porthcawl. Today they're having to deal with Hurricane Katia, or at least its remnants.

I too take refuge in The Buck. The woman's already sitting at the bar, looking thoughtful. But how often have I seen her? Too many times. Yet it's never easy to remember who she is.

Yes, let her be Katia. A change from the predictable

Keeley or Kayleigh. But she predates women with names like that, women marked with a K. Don't parents know that names starting with K are brandings, their owners scarred for life? Soon those names will be incomprehensible. From another language. Another era.

Still, I recognise her. Predictable on her barstool, one slip-on shoe hanging off, the mesh of her tights worn thin over a cracked heel. How do I know it's cracked? Because we are the same age and her heel is cracked where my heel is cracked and in need of a hard scrub. Digging where I dig, counting those ivory-coloured corals, round as moons, and walking where I walk, a pedicure seems urgent now. And when she stands it is as I do, one foot almost balancing on the other. A peculiar posture.

Yes, call her Katia. The hurricane woman. But that hurricane is almost blown out. Whenever I meet her, it is in places such as this. Always these places.

No matter the hour, time's nearly up. Katia knows it. Yet what else is there to do? Another drink? Another man? But all the men are lesser men now. Somehow disappointing men. Looking at such men she can measure herself. Gauge how far she has fallen. How far she has travelled in the wrong direction. Or she might compare herself to the others who are catching a different bus.

And as pubs will, The Buck encourages introspection. Iwan Llwyd wrote a poem about a man he met here. A man he considered a 'character'. Now Iwan is dead and that man still a drunken boor. I look at Katia, never so haggard, never more thoughtful. She glances at her watch and waits at the counter. The wind might have slackened and I leave.

3.

Two weeks later the town is full of men with tremendous quiffs and sideburns. Some of this hair is real. The first two I spotted were searching for a café. Yes, unmistakeable Elvis tributeers. Probably they had booked rooms a year in advance, Elvis weekend specials without breakfast.

And soon there are hundreds. And then thousands. Many are men and women dressed as Elvis, or characters in the Elvis pantheon. As this is particularly sparse for a man who recorded an (estimated) 800 songs, their fancy dress is given over not only to approximations of The King, but people wearing anything notionally historical from the period.

These include men turned out as GI's, with women as appropriate dancing partners, men and women dressed as 'hula' Elvis from the 'Hawaiian' films, adorned in plastic garlands. A few are characters salvaged from early hits like *Jailhouse Rock*.

This is one of the few songs that offer such opportunity. A Leiber-Stoller number from '57, Jerry Leiber died in August 2011 and was one of the era's better lyricists. Clearly he influenced Bob Dylan. 'Jailhouse Rock' offers drama, characterisation, wit. How rare.

Of those paying homage to Elvis, two or three members of one party are dressed as 'the Purple gang' – in fact "the whole rhythm section". There are also the convicts with their numbers, possibly Spider Murphy, Shifty, and 'the sad Sack'.

'Jailhouse Rock' and 'In the Ghetto' were probably the most interesting songs, lyrically, that Elvis recorded, the former ideal for interpretation by imaginative fancy-dressers.

Otherwise there are ironic, no, brutal commentaries on Elvis's weight gain in later years. Some men wear inflatable suits, others are padded with pillows. But generally, it's a bizarre parade. Anything goes, the weirder the better. Because tributes these days invariably involve some form of imperson-ation. Fancy dress has become a new art form.

Porthcawl seems an unlikely place for an Elvis celebration which has rapidly become extravagant. I work for the charity, Sustainable Wales, and am in the town every day. We have run a small shop for the last five years, *Sussed*, where all goods, the staff and volunteers are told, have their own unique story. We have to be able to tell those stories. So, be interested in what you sell, we encourage. This isn't an ordinary job. We're promoting life not a lifestyle.

That life might include local honey, environmentally-friendly detergent, fair trade chocolate. Crucial purchases? Hardly. We also sell new books. Not many, but enough to make us the only shop for miles aware of new literature.

But times are hard. The 'footfall' in Porthcawl, we're told, has declined dramatically. It seems that people are waiting for our first Tesco to open.

For the first Elvis festival we had taken our rare pink vinyl double album from 1978 – eighteen number ones and gatefold cover – to display in *Sussed*. Truthfully, it had rarely been played. Unlistenables included 'Love Me Tender', 'Don't Cry Daddy', 'Crying in the Chapel'. Mawkish, self-pitying, self-loathing.

That's why the best Elvis YouTubes show him drunk or overcome by absurdity. The highlight occurs when he heckles one of his backing singers. She misunderstands the purpose of his music, delivering an operetta-style performance. Sometimes, Elvis is saying, this is all… *ridiculous.*

And eight hundred and thirty seven Las Vegas concerts? Elvis's schedule seems preposterous but these days audiences for a single festival can be larger than his combined Vegas crowd. I was there when the Rolling Stones played Knebworth, August 21, 1976. They descended from a helicopter at 2 a.m., each an Orpheus with electric lyre, hair in spikes, tottering on Cuban heels.

The band faced down an audience estimated at half a million. Surely, they must have believed, they had been delivered into hell. When dawn broke, the scenes were apocalyptic. Knebworth, Woodstock, Isle of Wight? They were our generation's Waterloo. Or our Passchendaele. What a terrifying thought.

I admit I used to hate Elvis Presley. Didn't go to art school, did he? Wasn't in a group, was he? Importantly, he didn't write his own material, although he helped with early arrangements. Instead, he joined the army and was manipulated as a cash-cow by cynical management. John Lennon, who owed him so much ("before Elvis there was nothing") said joining up had castrated Elvis.

Yet I've changed. I still dislike most Elvis music, but the early raw rock and the late dramatic flourish are fine, the former because of reworkings of tunes such as 'Blue Moon over Kentucky'. These were propelled by a guitar and slapped bass played by Scotty Moore and Bill Black. The unreplicable Sun studio echo also contributed much. But most of those eight hundred songs are overwhelmed by kitsch. Formulaic, they're downright bad.

These days *Sussed* is the last shop in town where you might purchase new literature. Not that anyone does. How do book sellers manage? I've no idea. Books are fair trade chocolate in a world of Pound Shop bargain bins. In this town the last real book shop has given up and died. It will reopen as a hairdresser's, as everywhere else. I'm surprised the owners waited so long.

With the pink record I'd also taken the biography of Elvis by Albert Goldman. The album must have been noteworthy, as it was immediately stolen. The book was ignored, but then it is a hatchet job, almost literally so. Goldman's 600 pages have an unpleasant 'know-better-than-you' tone. It ends with a graphic account of Elvis's autopsy, and a list of the drugs present in the body. The complete report has been sealed until 2027, fifty years after Elvis's death.

Environmental purists look away now. In an attempt to make money out of the deceased, our idea for the festival was to turn our town centre office, known as 'The Green Room', into 'The Elvis Diner', offering coffee and sandwiches. We had thought particularly of 'The Elvis', assembled from a soft Italian loaf, a pound of peanut butter, several bananas cut lengthways, honey and a bacon garnish.

We also created a street stall for *Sussed* products, and played Elvis's music: scratchy vinyl, as authentic as we could manage. Raul Arieta, who runs the Porthcawl 'Rock Club' accompanied the songs, then played alone, R&B becoming freeform jazz. The rest of us danced. I'd like to say *jived* but jiving's beyond me, although my wife, who frequented the original Cavern, is adept. One music lover who heckled with cries of *wankers* was removed by the constabulary.

Yes, times are hard and the environmental movement financially embarrassed. The world now requires greens who are innovative entrepreneurs, maybe prepared to live with nuclear power. As the new austerity bites, so idealists seem fewer. Or am I simply bewildered by middle age?

Nevertheless, at *Sussed* we decided to do Elvis proud. The shop window displayed copies of the *Daily Mirror* front page from August 17, 1976 – "Elvis Presley is dead" – and old album sleeves, such as 'Aloha from Hawaii via Satellite' and 'Elvis Sings the Wonderful World Of Christmas'.

Dead, one man said to me. Don't you know he's only sleeping?

Like every other hero from history…

4.

Now town teems with men with impossibly black wigs and muttonchops. They are entrants in the festival's karaokes and competitions. And I ask, who are these people? Why have they come? The clearest answer is they hail from south Wales, especially the valleys, and the English Midlands. What they're creating is a magnificent working class eisteddfod. And whoever they are, they certainly understand the protocols of alcohol.

Thus the Elvis Festival is an excuse for drinking. Exactly the same as international rugby. But it's more subtly done. Thursday and Friday drinking constitute exquisite preliminaries. The booze is to be savoured, indeed relished, each glass deliciously anticipated.

Saturday drinking on the other hand is relentless and singleminded. The drinker is not merely owed his drink. He deserves it like no other drink he will take. This Saturday drinker propels himself determinedly into the amnesiac twilight of Sunday morning. The wreckage of Saturday night is spectacular.

Sunday's drinking has a wistful quality. Despite the regularity of Sabbath sport, a tracing of guilt adheres to it. The toasts are wry yet congratulatory. We survived last night, they seem to say. Don't know how. Don't know why...

For the Elvis Festival, drinking continued into Monday. This was a shifty, apologetic drinking, for which the drinker asked himself, why am I doing this? I didn't know I was allowed.

And Tuesday drinking? This is the *terra incognita* of booze. Yet I saw two men with cans of Special Brew together on a bench at Trinity. It was 9.30 a.m. and they were ready for the world. They too felt Porthcawl and Elvis owed them a drink. Perhaps we did.

5.

Saturday night it rains torrentially. But I'm out with plenty of others, not all of whom are inebriates, looking for buses amongst unfamiliar fleets. We're soaked but there's a definite camaraderie.

What would Elvis have done? someone asks, joining a bus queue.

Get a taxi, comes a reply.

Before I go I pass the breakwater. Surely nobody would be rash enough to venture there? But yes, a hesitant figure has blundered on, looking for the right road.

He won't find it there. It's a dangerous place to walk, along a narrow stone pier where the lighthouse glows a spectral orange through its panes.

Better take care, Elvis, I say to the legions surrounding me. Better take care.

As to Katia, I've forgotten what she looks like. Yet I know I will see her again.

Infinity Speaker

Homage to Guillevic
(1907-1997)

Avebury

The stars are running down the avenues of Avebury. I look through the stones at the comets and sphinx-faced Mars, at the cartoons of the constellations and all the familiar cosmic crowd. And together we gaze down the avenues of Avebury, seeking the energy stored in its cells, that battery that burns under the wheat and the wheat-coloured flints and the sunken coliseums of chalk.

Down these white roads I go, and think: do stones wait? Are these stones waiting? Perhaps for some summons from the ones they will recognise, and though weak as the brain's electricity, a fire will race between them.

But is Avebury waiting? Screwed into their sockets like grey light bulbs these stones are a religion abandoned by priests grown tired of waiting. So I listen to rooks, those cinders in the sunset, and the power lines above the Red Lion, crackling with our prayers.

Now here is January asleep under its webbing, an army dreaming of what it means to win a war.

At the stones it is soon midnight. This one I touch as if it was a child. How easily the frost's pixels vanish under my hand. For this next stone there's a formal embrace, but surely this next is already a lover, my tongue in the bell of its armpit, and I know the salt of it, the pulse, the stone's body ivoried in the lights of the A4.

And when I look, there is my skin upon Avebury's skin, my heart against Avebury's heart, and here is my thinking against Avebury's thinking and my snow upon the snow of Avebury, trodden to transparency. Six thousand Januaries of snow under my heels.

The four thousand at Carnac

Once again
what shall we do with you,
those of us who are able?

Upright in the sun,
proud of our labours,
always approaching a greater secret,

And you, our remorse
for not having gained it. *

A minute ago they were mine. Those footprints. A minute ago the cressbeds, a commotion of cormorants – augers of the tide. A minute ago those footprints were mine. On the quayside, on the river-riven stones those footprints leading up to me. Were mine. Leading to the quayside and the cressbeds. Those. Mine. A minute ago. Leading up to me. On the river-riven stones.

Modern poetry resembles a party in some overheated apartment. Everyone talks, nobody listens. Guillevic is invited but has not arrived. Or has he? Who is that then, looking out of the window? What's to see?

In a line of iron pines there's an oak. And a red squirrel. And there are *Les Geants de Kerzerho*, menhirs splintered by lightning, a little removed from the crowd.

We have forgotten the reasons for these four thousand stones. Perhaps they are a dance. An architecture. A language. But I wonder how we could have mislaid what seems now the most important knowledge in the world.

Appetite intervenes. I carry a tray of oysters through the town and serve them with lemon, a redflecked loaf and *cidre fermier* from Vergers de Kermabo, at a table where two rivers join.

Bloody stones, we splutter. Maybe they're an alphabet. Or telephone boxes.

Yet one thing's clear. They were important once and are more so now. Those stones. Grey as the barley under a megalithic sky. Yet my mind tracks back to the blackthorn born this morning.

Mwr

On the train they look like us. Sober in charcoal, plugged into Playstations. Or in their Izuzu Warriors on the Tonysguboriau sliproad, Bridge FM in the Infinity speakers.

But when they come home it's different. They hang their Samsungs on the sea-rocket and in the oystershells still used as mirrors they regard themselves. At last, the weekend. At last they can relax. And speak their own language.

These people are the neolithics. There are not many left but there were few to start. Rather short. A little stocky. So they blend in as they always have.

And that language? Highly endangered. In fact it's down to one word. That word is *mwr*. But don't ask what mwr means. Mwr might mean a million things. Breadcrumb sponge? That's mwr. Moon jelly? Mwr will do. Downsize? Throughput? Must be mwr. Because mwr is all these people need to build a life. To continue a civilisation. As to losing words, they're used to it. *Mws* and *mwth*? *Morkin* and *mormo*? They came and went. Words are mortal too.

But to me mwr was always a puzzle. I've heard the word for thirty years. And forgotten I hear it. So I thought I'd solve its mystery.

On a day without colour, fog like deadwhite pearls of arsenic, I asked the watchmen in the bonded warehouse, their backs to the brandies and the baldaquins, to the chalices turned from Brazilian bloodwood.

Their eyes were on their cards, then on the dealer, then scanning a screen where nothing moved. No-one murmured of mwr in that place. There were rottweilers that stood over thimbles of myrrh but of miracles there was no mind.

When I came out I looked at the water. Something was moving, maybe a wreck the current nudged. Yes maybe mwr was there. But I wandered back inland around the bends in Briton's Way.

I asked a man digging into a dunghill but he shook his head.

There's no such word, he muttered, and returned to the wall of mauve and cream he had exposed in the midden, cutting at that seam, his own misery sufficient, his blade faith enough.

In her driveway a woman was polishing a powerboat's nameplate and she laughed and said that she was a newcomer to the country and did not care for its murky corners.

In the schoolyard my old headmaster looked morose.

Did we teach you nothing? he asked. Or is it so easy to forget? We murdered mwr, we made it meagre, a field, a ditch, a name too strange for the map, a morsel the surveyors spared, a moor behind locked doors.

He's wrong, I thought as I came away. The histories say nothing but I know there will be more to mwr tomorrow, that mwr is the mirror of a marvellous vale, an outpost, an outcrop, a forest, a fortress and on the atlas's last page mwr is a moraine with the moonlight's electroplate upon it, a city under the sand, a monument, a battlefield, an isthmus slim as an avocet's ankle, a reef, a rift, a rendezvous in the corner of the graveyard where the babies are buried with no-one to mourn and the graves are thrown open like music boxes where our names are played once and are gone.

Yes I guess that is mwr. Or Mwr. A muster of ghosts. But in the meantime I will go back to the sea, to what was moving there, and sit in The Marine on a corner stool amongst a gang of myrmidons sipping malt and we will muse on the merits of a single syllable and wager the wheres and whens of it and the homecoming we shall have.

---

* *Translation of this poem from Guillevic's 'Carnac' by Teo Savory, from 'Selected Poems' Penguin (1974). See also Bloodaxe's 'Selected Poems' of Guillevic (1999).*

Old Man of the Willow

There's a knock on the door. Wes comes in with a box under his arm.

Thought you'd like to see this, he says.

Thanks, Wes.

This one's a beauty. Oh yes.

Seen one before, Wes. West of here.

Thought you'd like to see.

He's a beauty all right, I say.

Fourth time. No. Make it five.

But only roadkill.

Fifth time I caught this one.

On the highway, I say. Going down to Druid.

Yip. Five times.

Side of the road. I stopped and looked at it.

Had this box handy.

Coming out of some town up there.

Cardboard box.

Black and white. Like this one. Smaller though. Coming out of Dodsland it might have been.

Lost his wife, this one has.

And the ants were busy.

And his kits long gone. Caught him sweet as shelling peas. Fifth time.

You're the best, Wes.

Won't learn, see. Won't learn their lessons.

No road sense either.

Follow their bellies is what they do. Greedy SOBs.

Yeah. Seen one before, Wes. Maybe in Druid.

Reckon I'll drive him this time. Ten miles say. Drive him.

Good idea, Wes.

Yeah. Ten miles. Let him out in country.

Or could have been Super.

Wes puts down the box. It's a Monterey Jack cardboard box with the panels parted. I look in again.

It could eat its way out of there, says Wes.

Maybe, I say. But it knows the game's up.

Know what kills one?

What?

Fisher. Bites his nose. Flips him over and unzips his belly.

I look again. This one understands. From his sett it regards the world with one black eye. The turning world. So many changes. Yes there it squats with muscles like velvet rippling under its spines. Its cowl of thorns. I look at its eye. The biggest blackest button from the button box. But it won't look at me. It turns its head. I'm too strange. It turns its head at the sight of my face. Turns round in the box like a dog in snow.

Thought you'd like to see.

Thanks, Wes.

And Wes puts the panels back and squats down beside the box, Wes with his liverspots, his ballcap that says Margaretville Bun & Cone.

Could have been Super, I say.

This time is the last time, sighs Wes.

He's a beauty.

Getting to be a habit.

A real beauty.

Course, says Wes standing up. I could get the axe.

The axe?

Well, yeah. You know. The axe.

I crouch down and open the panels and look at the quills, thick as drinking straws. They ripple as if the wind was blowing. A current in the corn.

Then I close the box and pick it up. I pass the box to Wes.

No, I say. Leave the axe. Take him up to Super, Wes. Take him back to Plenty.

The Key to Annie's Room

1.

It was an annexe stained by cigarette smoke. The furniture was one table and two chairs. There was a blackboard and a whitepainted Michelin X tyre cut in half attached to the wall. Within the tyre was a dartboard.

Behind the counter the landlord kept a set of three: plastic flights, dimpled brass alloy barrels. The whole room seemed to have been attacked by woodworm. Then suddenly it was league rules and game on.

2.

To live in Wales is to be conscious at dusk of the football results. We have created a country where sport is not only a healthy pastime but an obsession and a dread. Every media orifice releases an effluvium of prognostications and inquests.

Goal difference, try count, run chase bewitch the talk jockeys. Ataraxia? Didn't they play Wrexham once in the Inter-Toto Cup? And the results, a global tinnitus, are inescapable. Heard the score? someone asks. You'll never believe it.

You'd better believe it. Especially about rugby. If sport is a sickness, there is something malarial about rugby. Night sweats, daylight delirium, the tongue's anarchy. And every year the fever is deeper, its season more prolonged. I can say this as a player and a spectator. And increasingly as a sufferer.

Because today in Wales, rugby inflicts itself more profoundly on our lives than ever before. Sport in general and rugby in particular has crept up the pecking order of the television news. Only a decade ago, sport and the weather were the concluding items. Today they often lead.

What makes rugby ultimately absurd is the seriousness surrounding it: the training; the fitness 'regimes', its work ethic. Scrum *machines*? Do they gouge, lift or talk back? Can they go to a nightclub?

Recently I watched the Ospreys-Toulouse game in the European Championship. The home team was led out by a seven foot shark in a duffle coat. The surrealism continued as the wind and rain roiled in the west. Quickly the players became Papuan mudmen. First they seemed comical, then inept. It was an important game but there was virtually no crowd. These were our heroes, at the peak of professionalism, coached, motivated, yet undone by a force seven over Mumbles Head. They might have been playing in a carwash. What did it all mean?

Rugby's most obvious victim is the capital city. On match days it closes down. Undoubtedly, Cardiff requires sport. But intelligent sport. It needs the on-field dazzle that the marble edifices of the Bay and the adamantine cockscomb of the St. David's Hotel are bestowing on its architecture. But during last autumn's Rugby World Cup it was a no-go area for anyone not wishing to get Heinekened out of their heads in its café bars. For those who ventured in, there was one occupation. Punditry, whilst looking at wraparound screens as our players hit the Millennium turf. Joining the throng, I made surreptitious notes. But whilst wanting to describe the present, I was constantly tugged back by the stars of my own era.

The Quinnells? Now I understand why France will never allow British beef back into the country. Scott Gibbs? Robocop on amphetamines. And as the matches progressed, Rob Howley cut an alarming figure. A vast poster was erected in Cardiff, courtesy of BT. With every game the poster seemed to become bigger. Howley's haunted eyes and hollow cheeks towered over the city. The age of anxiety had arrived.

Something dreadful was about to happen. Here was a Big Brother losing his grip and according to the *Western Mail*, his 'world class' status recently bestowed by that same paper's posse of rugby writers.

So what about Jenks? Of those 300 international penalties. That world record. Yes, our millennial monument to tedium. Three hundred penalties mean four hundred and fifty minutes of the nation holding its breath like some bizarre cult suicide. (Models of the points-scoring boot are now on eBay. One hundred and five quid to you, butty.) But at least Jenkins looks human. Note how most international threequarters have become indistinguishable from one another – an overmuscled species of genetically-enginered mercenary, all snarling gumshields and bodybuilders' stretchmarks. But that does not include Allan Bateman.

I remember Bateman as permanently aged 35. Usually, he's injured. This only underlines his superior wisdom. On the rare occasions he does don the corporate Welsh shirt he's as cunning as a conger. Or at least someone who can run and think at the same time. If rugby was chess, Bateman would be both bishop and knight. He is equally adroit at taking the thrilling diagonal and the perplexing counter direction. Catch him while you can.

Finally, there is the Boss. Graham Henry has been nicknamed The Great Redeemer. He is invited to schools and hospitals to encourage. To bless. Very quickly he has learned that the Welsh are paralysed by lack of self confidence. One recurring image of this abjectness is their enthusiasm for tough-talking, wry-smiling father-figures. Admonition, then a hug. I love you, daddy. As an ex-headmaster with a nimbus of All Black macho mystique about him, Henry fitted the bill. He broods high in the stand, frowning so deeply it seems he has glimpsed a future in which Wales loses to the Blasket Islands and an Ikea XV. Around him sits the masonry of the WRU committees. Smug as ampersands.

Henry quickly learned that the Welsh are at their best in

crowds. Individually, they lack the cultural grit of the Irish, the exasperating gene of English authoritarianism. But communal cockiness quickly palls. Not finding sufficiently talented players in Wales, Henry trawled the old dominions for wild blood, adventurers who might leave home for piratical challenges at Rodney Parade and Westgate Street. His stricture is clear. It is easy to paint your face red and green and queue for two hours in the Millennium Stadium for a three quid can of Happy Shoppa lager. Easy and horribly explicit.

The coach became aware of the depth of this problem on his first flight into Cardiff airport. Greeting the world's travellers is a statue of the greatest Welshman. Who might that be? Aneirin Bevan, of inspirational political vision? Iolo Morgannwg, who was telling us two hundred years ago that there was too much reality about? No. It is Gareth Edwards. How could we forget those tries, repeated again and again? Who would allow us to forget?

Welsh people, Henry has repeated, need to learn how to stand apart from the throng. (Which, to be fair, is what Edwards did. As a player he was usually greater than his team.) Where, demands the boss, is the Wales of the imagination? Quit the flock. Write your own lines instead of accepting the bitpart offered by social orthogenesis. Yes, but it's hard, Mr Henry. It's so hard.

To be fair, it is the media, especially the *Western Mail*, that are responsible for the hyperbole that bloats rugby and anaesthetises everything else. This newspaper has devoted hundreds of thousands of words, all instantly forgotten, to ligaments, 'super twelves' and 'crises'. There have been more crises in Welsh rugby than the Balkans. Television coverage doesn't help. I would prefer to remember Jonathan Davies as an angel dancing on a pinhead, than as a pundit with nothing to say and saying it in a voice like a glove-puppet. I admired Ray Gravelle when he practiced genuine Stradey piraticism. Today he's become an all-purpose factotum for cultural orthodoxy: S4C, the gorsedd, rugby as mystical rite. On the other hand I'd rather encounter Dai "The Enforcer" Young in his Top Man togs than a red jersey, headband pulled tight, eyes bulging like an extra from *Human Traffic*.

Thus, after speaking to devotees at Walkabout and The Scrum, my recommendations are:

* Realise that rugby is about money and not nationality. So? Ban the national anthems. The players' tears and American-style fists on hearts are cringeworthy to those of us who thought John Redwood word perfect throughout *Mae hen wlad*. Instead, play the sponsors' company songs.

* Turn the game on its side. The World Cup was five weeks of piled up juggernauts. The jags and mercs were stuck in traffic. All I recall are behemothian backsides wiggling under the daylight moon above the Millennium Stadium. So? If the touchlines became the trylines and vice versa, there would be more points and greater space for the wings. Remember Dewi Bebb, the ghost who smelt of wintergreen? Or Gerald's snipeflight through a misty afternoon? John Bevan's buffalo soldiering? JJ like a red stamen of mercury? Turn the game on its side and we'll see their like again. And the crowd will have a better view.

* Ensure everyone who plays for Wales comes from Ponty. We'd lose the matches but win the brawls in the nightclubs afterwards. And that's where it really counts.

3.

A Dutch hell's angel in frightwig and marmalade vest inches through the crowd. He bears a tray of *oranjeboom*, fizzing and deadly. Finding a corner table he waves in delight at the tv camera. *Jah*, he mimes. Six pints. And all for me. *Tot straks*.

Now we're getting there. Sports coverage increases exponentially to fill the media time available to it. Digital television has encouraged further efflorescence. Meanwhile, on BBC, sport has reached the pinnacle of the news hierarchy. We are all Man United fans now. If Wales loses a Six Nations match it must devastate both the individual and the national psyche. Caring is compulsory. But as the digital labyrinth convolves, we will need to identify where our loyalties lie.

Mine are with darts. I rediscovered darts at this year's World Championships, held in the cathedral-sized lounge of the Lakeside Country Club, Frimley Green. The last darts I had played was in that ciborium in a Bridgend hotel, decades previously. The longest sums I'll ever write. At Frimley, English, Welsh and Dutch fans cwtched together in the sparkling alcoholic fug. Tuxedoed hosts explained the poetry of scoring. A 120 to finish required a Shanghai. A measley 1 meant the darter had entered The Madhouse or Annie's Room. Then, on to the stage, stepped Count Dracula. A beergutted demigod in black lurex, The Count tossed plastic vampire bats into the audience. He next proceeded to lay low The Archer, sponsored by a firm of West of England meatpackers, in a match classified by darting elders as 'epic'.

Throughout the tournament the aristocracy of darts had looked in for a swift half and photo opp. In real life they were publicans or scraped by on the exhibition circuit, throwing backwards or indian-style. All were paragons of numeracy. One hundred and thirty seven check-out? The third dart would be airborne before the crowd could lift another frenchfry. And as ever in the tournament, the players' flash wives exhorted their partners like marine sergeants, faking every orgasmic 180, tamping their glasses, straining in dresses tight as the green foil over dew-encrusted Pils.

And when The Count had climaxed with a perfect 170 and sunk to his knees, union jack flights still quivering where his last arrow lay against the bullseye wire, the crowd launched into its planned delirum. Dutchman hugged Englishman. A Welshman in rugby shirt, carrying an inflatable sheep, mobiled the bar for a gargantuan round.

Yes, darts is the answer. There's more booze in it than rugby but none of the gloating nationalism. As long as we beat the English we don't care? Yeah, right. In darts, everyone understands that the prelibations and inquests that stretch an eighty minute rugby international into a week of onanistic dreariness could never apply to their sport.

Darts is not serious. Darts is amateur dramatics with tungsten tips. Because it's as camp as a pantomime horse, darts remains uninfected by self importance. It is not a subject for mass delusion or a specious metaphor for identity and belonging. And there are no bluejawed loose-heads threatening mayhem. On the oche, sport returns to human scale. Down that four metre corridor can be found natural redemption through modesty and loss. Because darts acknowledges its own risibility, it will never be involved with the puerile messianics of the back page. Those fascistic longings. Well, that's what Annie told me. And she should know.

A Dream of the Tortoise

*A meditation by Alfonsina Storni on Jorge Luis
Borges and the suburbs of Buenos Aires*

There was a house I used to pass on the street named
Arevalo. Number 2378, if I recall. A long street, you would
think, but not so long for Palermo or for Baires itself, that city
of long streets and longer afternoons.

It was a heavy door, of some tropical wood. Maybe
rosewood or mahogany. On my wanderings I would look
forward to reaching that door, so immense yet welcoming.
But I never dreamed to knock. It was enough to look at the
door itself. Because what a satisfying thing is a door. What an
irrevocable statement a door makes.

One day, one afternoon that is, for once it was always
afternoon in Palermo, I happened to be there again. I found
myself dreaming through the slumber of Palermo, the
shadows of the plane trees my only companions, the dust
glinting in the gutters, when the door opened. The wonderful
door. And through the door came a blonde woman. Of
course, I had to look. To stare.

A blonde woman in Palermo? Impossible, I thought. What
is she, a Swede, a German in a city that was soon to know
many Germans? But at that time she seemed unique. In the
city of the dark machismo.

And behind the blonde woman came a tall man. A man as
tall as the woman was blonde. And the man carried a camera,
one of those expensive cameras, hooded like a falcon. I
imagined its lens the navy blue of a newborn's eye. An

awkward contrivance, that camera, borne with both hands. And the woman walked by and we exchanged pleasantries in Castellano, and I was rewarded with a glimpse into the hallway before the man closed the door.

At the hall's end was a harpsichord. Yes, I'm certain of that. Because there was another man who sat at the harpsichord and played. I caught a few notes. Bach, I'm sure. The key of E major, the sunlit key. The key of hope and maybe of redemption. Yes, I heard a stave or two, might even have improvised my own phrases. And then the door closed on the house of harpsichords. For that's what I called it from then on: 2378 Arevalo, the house of harpsichords. Because harpsichords make the music of the afternoon. Especially of the waking dreams of what were Palermo afternoons.

After meeting the blonde woman, I went more frequently along that street. But I never saw her there again, or the man with the camera. And I never heard the harpsichord except in my head. E major on a silent afternoon, with horse dung in the middle of the road and a dusty Phaeton parked under the planes. Maybe a hummingbird poised motionless, kissing the air; the way a hummingbird hangs like a model of a hummingbird. Little jade ornament of the somnolent hours.

I tell you this because I happened to be there this week. Yes I, Alfonsina Storni, sixty years after my death, in Palermo once again. Not that my behaviour was so different. I found myself drifting past, as light as that hummingbird I could exactly recall. Its scarlet bill fine as a hypodermic. Its invisible wings. Yes, an E major moment in the afternoon light.

There was the house. If this was Arevalo, it had to be the same residence. But where was the door? The wonderful door with its carvings and brass knocker had been wrenched from its frame. A new door, a hateful and insignificant door, an atrocity of a door, stood in its place. And the spaces in the porch were filled with shoddy brickwork.

Yet, I said – to myself of course – because who else might I speak to now? It doesn't matter anymore. At least to me.

But I walked on, turning right out of Arevalo, into the traffic and crowds of what felt a different district. And I drifted down Santa Fe, and there were others who floated with me, shadows like myself, but we were few compared to the bustle of the avenidas. And I came eventually home to the trees. To the patio where I linger.

And now, for this moment, it's the end of our expedition. Because we've reached the park in Palermo and I must stay here with the boys. The very big boys. Because the poets are remembered here. At least that hasn't changed so much. The poets loved Palermo and now in its turn Palermo loves its poets. And I am with them, for was I not a poet? My last poem was published in *La Nacion,* and while the public read it over coffee and medialunas, or in the swinging omnibus, I was stepping into a river as wide as an ocean.

Yes, here in the park we are a fine group of faces. Not such a bad ending. Perhaps honour at last. This is my kind of fame. I'm with Casona and Machado. And Lorca. Poor Lorca. Not far away is Asturias, the Guatemalan, whom I have never read, despite his Nobel. Yes, he's the copper-headed laureate whose brow in this summer light is too hot for the children to touch. Ah, the irony of that. Because Borges is here too, old JLB, Borges who was never Nobeled, Borges with his bust wrapped in sackcloth. For restoration they say. Well, they are taking their time. But I am here with Borges and he with me.

You know Borges? The new Palermo is filled with Borges. He is its industry. The tourists flock to read the postcards of his poems. *Oh destiny of Borges, perhaps no stranger than your own.* How they shiver when they read those lines. The writer musing on mortality as the readers contemplate their own likely fate and fame.

But I prefer it here to Mar del Plata. I stand there also in stone, befitting the point of my departure. Yes I like it here under the trees, or on the Patio d'Andaluz, a recent gift of Spain but already starting to crumble. The patio is roped off to the public but no-one sees me wander the turquoise steps. Its water chimes like bells. And such shade. A jaguar's dappling.

Now, didn't Borges write that the name of the faceless god who waits behind the other gods, the real god's secret name, consists of fourteen words? And are not those fourteen words written in the black and golden fur of the jaguar? How typical of the man. With his mysteries and his sects and his cod learning. A schoolboy thrilling over an atlas. He never grew up. And yet I enjoy the shadows here. Close to the poets and their bronze agonies.

Yes, I smile to myself. What would JLB have made of the new Palermo? Something marvellous perhaps. Borges dealt in symbols, of course. In magic and universes alternate to our own. So what would Borges have thought of what I noticed today, wandering Palermo. It was a disorderly line of plump, no, enormous people, outside the office of Endemol Argentina, on the once quiet street of Ravignani.

Endemol is not a drug. Or perhaps it is. And it sounds like the name of an angel. But this Endemol makes television programmes, such as *Big Brother*. Oh yes, I know all about Big Brother. As I speak, there are riots in India, the burning of effigies, because of Endemol's *Big Brother*. The whole world is watching television now. We must all be famous. We must all immerse ourselves in celebrity's acid bath.

But these are people the like of whom I had never seen in Palermo. People wider than the borracho tree. People who suppose themselves fat. Yes, fat. People who believe they qualify for society's definition of obese. And yes, it makes sense. In a world devoted to the carnality of the emaciated, they strike a strident poise. These must be the new revolutionaries, the new poets. But even I, who was once deemed plain, and sturdy, cannot approve.

For these people believe they have found a role. A meaning. These people stand patiently for a reality show audition for fat people.

Reality? I could tell them about reality. The shadow of the schirrus in the veins of the breast. Mar del Plata muddy to the knee. To the neck. Yet there are so many of them, or they are so enormous, that they stop the traffic. A policeman comes and scratches himself. Because Endemol has sent out its summons, its clarion through cyberspace for extreme people. For fat people. For people who are so large they will stop traffic. The hour of the grotesque has arrived.

As for Borges, who was not so svelte himself, he would have asked, is this procession at Ravignani 1470, the fat people's dream, the company's dream, or our own dream of fat people? Who is dreaming whom here? Under the plane trees. Beside the borracho. For surely this cannot be Baires. In the Club Eros and Bar el Gallego where the *tallerines con tuco*, the *matambre*, the *chorizo de lomu* might make us all immense, the diners remain slim as street cats.

Just look at these two. *Cartoneros* they call them in the new Palermo: two slim, liquid sifters of rubbish. In another world, the coming world of Endemol, they will be models, languid upon their divans, irretrievably ignorant. In the stone-coloured light of the Endemolian infra-red they will sleep a dreamless sleep. Yet here in the capital, for the moment that remains to us, they are anonymous street sweepers, collectors of cardboard and Sprite bottles, riders of the rubbish lorry like children on a hay cart. How dark they are, their skin dirty as centavos. They live in shacks, make love on concrete shelves behind the bus station.

Orchids I call them and I salute their lives, I who was offered no favours and who once sang in a café lit the colour of sour wine while the poets turned their heads to the street.

3pm. The exhausted hour. But it's less the afternoons now. My moment is midnight. Night time Palermo means neon and the chrome of cockroaches; a glass of Fernet's bitter fern, that vertiginous vermouth, abandoned on a bar. While the traffic of ghosts is stilled.

My Palermo is the insomnia of eternity. And the plane

trees? Mottled like those street cats. I used to think such trees diseased. As pale as leprosy? Yes, the English poet who wrote that knew what derangement meant.

Now, let's move again. Let's extend our promenade. And look where we are. Even I find this hard to credit. It is Jorge Luis Borges Street. Poor Palermo? I don't think so. Its afternoons are busier now, its heyday at hand. And that too will pass. But yes, poor Borges. Did we ever meet? Hardly. The older woman's is an impossible role, too excruciating for your worst enemy.

Sometimes I thought him a salamander. More often a tortoise under the reading light. Yes, the tortoise of old Palermo. Yet, some aspects of life remain unchanged. I still see the virgins in the tango bars going to hell on a sunbeam. But now the *porteños* sit in Sushi Libre and Starbucks. The American developers are here: beggars with Blackberries. The fight is on. The twin ziggurats of Hollywood are already constructed.

In Bar el Gallego, the owner has written on the wall *'la ultima de Baires resiste en Palermo Hollywood'*. Such is their defiance. And sometimes I too sit in El Gallego, at three or four in the afternoons when there is only an old man with a plate of crumbs or a group of business types lingering over a bottle of Torrentes. But one morning, drifting by, I was sure I saw the blonde woman, the man with a camera, in a far corner, there for breakfast, talking to a waiter in the new Lunfardo.

But of course not. It is many years since I visited the house of harpsichords. And then I thought, yes, it is possible. Because once, didn't the tortoise write of 'witnessing', of the death of the last witness at Christ's crucifixion?

What was lost from the world, he asked, when that witness died? And of himself? What will die with me when I die? he wrote. What will become extinct? Borges could find little more than the image of a roan horse in the vacant lot at Serrano and Charcas. And yes, here we are now. Where

Charcas, now called *Borges*, meets Serrano.

Is there a horse? I look around. And maybe even a ghost can gasp. There are, in fact, two horses, with jacaranda in their manes, pulling a tourist carriage. How peculiar. But a vacant lot? No. A pharmacy and some flats. But at 2154, or is it 2156, here is a house called *Casa del Maestro*.

Is that where JLB lived? I cannot remember. Not everything remains clear. But *maestro*? Maybe. Let's give him that. It would have pleased his mother and his two belated wives. But especially it pleases Palermo.

Close to the end, I whispered to my son who was also my companion. The world is over, I told him. This is it. Time has run away from me, Alfonsna Storni, the poet, the professor, run faster than a Rivadavia tram. Not that Baires was all of my life. Didn't I see the foal born in the pasture, the dam biting its neck to make it rise? And a girl entering a cactus-wood confessional to whisper her shame?

Yet now it occurs, perhaps Borges was correct after all. Perhaps all this is one of old JLB's dreams, a dream of the tortoise, the tortoise that wins the race. Because as he says himself, if the tortoise starts first, none of us will ever catch up. Never Achilles. Never the hare.

Dear listener, my problem was Argentine men. They were either wolves or waifs. That was the choice. After a while I gave up trying to salvage something from the masses in their mackintoshes who crowded every evening into the trams, rushing away from what they hated, to lives they never understood.

Men in their cafes. Always their cafes. The water glass, the napkin, the eye of coffee dark as a doe's. And men forever in groups, their heads together over the table, impenetrable as a thorn bush. Safety in numbers.

So when I lifted my eyes who could meet my gaze? Yes, they turned their faces when I stood up to recite because my voice was greater than theirs and inhabited a region they had never visited. Recite? I declaimed in whispers. I thundered like the humming bird. But did Borges ever enjoy my poems? He forgot to say.

So what did his learning amount to if it burned out his eyes? What is celebrity when a 62-year old man must be escorted by his mother on a lecture tour of Texas? Of all places. Why didn't he take some *chica*, some immodest scholar who could ignore raised eyebrows? And what's intelligence when the woman a man worships shrivels unwoo'd, unwed? If that's what she cares about. Oh destiny of Borges. Perhaps no stranger than my own.

In a Rainforest

The map was unforgiving. Surely there were no kin or kind of mine in those hills. But I went on, a moon over the passing places and Saturn in the pawnbroker's window.

Soon on both sides the valleys were black cisterns, the only colour where loggers bled the spruce of their gold.

The rest was slate. Even the sun was slate. And slate-eyed the roadagents who swarmed in that place. But how quickly it was evening when light split like slate, slats and slits of it, and the stars too, slate-coloured and screwed into their slots.

So whose was the face under the slate lintel of the schoolhouse? I swear I saw her. The parting in her hair a comet's trail. That woman, they said, had paced her room for thirty years. Slight her silhouette. A sloven they said. Disconsolate slut. Yet I saw a saint desolate in her desire.

No kin to me. No kind. But on I went under the ash trees' slatey buds, slate on my tongue and slate dust in my shoes, the people too, sharp as slate and all its angles, their language megaliths in my mouth.

Then next morning there was the river and where the slate was blue the water was green and where the slate was green the water was black and where the slate was black the water was sharp as shellac or purple as Aberangell eels.

So I stopped there. Climbed a wall and topped a stile, followed a rope ladder through the wood along the riverbank, came to a cord someone had tied around the trees. That they might escape. To tell the tale. And I went on.

To find myself sniffing the air. To feel myself a polecat in that place, a marten maybe, some creature back from the brink. Because I had unextincted myself. I was alive and there I stood, a being with eyes closed, my blood the hot circuit of honeysuckle that hung from the hurdles of the wood.

And that was where I stooped to drink, my mouth to the moss and moschatel, a vineland of water that waystation, the trees humming like pylons as I sipped sap, the rain a bead and bezel in every web.

What were the others there? Ticks, leeches, dewcats. But I looked harder. There was a light. On I went towards that glow to find a glade lit like a sick room. And there they were. Waiting for me. For two thousand years they had waited and now I had arrived. The rendezvous was made.

Where the dead are coral and coal the corpseflowers grow. Here they sprouted from Ordovician hearts and wombs. Many bodies must have lain under the trees: Romans who hadn't turned back, children deaf to warnings, coffins from the cholera graves slipped down the hill of knives from Corris.

And what flowers. Mauve and white, set like teeth on the trunks, and in such luxuriance they might have been undisturbed for centuries.

What else? Bryony on its abacus, orchids with their mirrors and mascara. But I had eyes only for the corpseflowers.

An offertory of candles they seemed to me. Flames of the marsh gas, prehistoric pilot lights, as around us the slate settled itself, its darkness infiltrating the delirious dew.

Then my foot touched a twmp. There was a rail under the mulch, the drum of a dram wheel. Maybe a station name. This was where the trains had come, opening up the country, bringing the settlers in and the slate out, that slate cut and dressed in the cliff's quarto, the last of it now left slewed in the slough, with me in slomo slummocking back to the road.

nok, nok, nokia on Heaven's Door: the Outlook from Helsinki

Football? The last time I had anything to do with football was sharing a lift with Ryan Giggs.

We were staying at a hotel in Tirana. He held a pair of muddy boots and stared at the floor as around him American voices on a UN mercy mission talked about afforestation and the turbidity of local red wine.

Outside, dictatorship was deceased. In its place, young and exceedingly raw capitalism was bringing its own brand of savagery to the streets of the Albanian capital. Giggs had missed a sitter in the national stadium, and Wales hung on for a 1-1 draw with Europe's leading emerging nation. Emerging from the hermetic isolation and the paranoid fantasies of its recent past. Emerging perhaps from purgatorial poverty. But not emerging, it transpired, from the culture of the blood feud or the rituals of ethnic violence.

Five years later, I picked up the microphone. It was a midsummer midnight in Lahti, one hundred kilometres north of Helsinki. The sky was the colour of vodka. It was my job to commentate on a Finland versus Rest-of-the-World soccer match. Two hundred voices roared the Finns on but within ten minutes they were 4-0 down. In that dusk-dawn whiteness the players slipped like phantoms amongst the birch trees. Fearing the result would plunge the spectators into stereotypical national gloom, I urged them not to drown their sorrows in the nearby lake.

At half time, fifteen minutes into the match and comprising a pause for a couple of bottles of Koff, this commentator was substituted. At full time, Finlandia's midnight sons had lost 7-4. They toasted their humiliation in Russian champagne.

The soccer players were writers. For a week every two years, Lahti teems with journalists and literary types brought together from around the world to discuss a 'theme'. Our theme on that occasion was 'literature is the enemy of stupidity'. But first we had to agree on what constituted such an opponent.

Most delegates agreed stupidity could be a good thing. In the right circs. Was not stupidity light, playful, ironic, iconoclastic, even wise in the manner of Good Soldier Schweik, or Shakespeare's fools, or Peter Sellers' character in *Being There*? (Perhaps we should cut the Sellers)

And wasn't stupidity a useful tool for anarchists everywhere, though perhaps not the Black Block 'anarchists' of the protests at Prague, Goteborg and subsequently Genoa. Indeed, was not stupidity *clever* in many respects?

This was where delegates (well, this one) equated stupidity with accelerating globalisation. Didn't such globalisation, I enquired, endanger cultural and economic as well as ecological variety? Didn't such a process engender the *stupidities* of uniform appetite and aspiration? And were not the symbols of that stupidity, such as the global brands of Gap, McDonald's, Pepsi, as visible in Lahti as Los Angeles.

I pressed on in that company of scribes. If McDonald's was responsible for environmental damage and poor health, if a paper plate of Chicken McNuggets had become a talisman for millions of upwardly mobile Chinese, if Nike and its globalising consortia represented Western culture at its nadir, weren't the stupidities of the consumerist machine yet marketed with genius? If nothing was crummier, nothing was cleverer.

Such was the paradox of our globalised world. At least, so it appeared on that undarkenable day. Because there is nothing cleverer than this type of stupidity. This stupidity understands its enemies are imagination, independence, curiosity, self-sufficiency.

Too simple, came the response. Globalisation was not necessarily a means of dumbing down. Or of controlling society. Globalisation had gone on in Europe since Latin grew its tree of languages, since religion took to reproducing itself, since the expeditions west out of the blue Tagus.

And forget McDonald's, someone said. A McWorld does not necessarily mean a McMind. America's totalitarian kitchens are the least of our problems. The godfathers of globalisation were Jesus Christ and Mohammed. English and Spanish were its midwives. Then came the combustion engine, the microchip. And now gene technology.

Globalisation? We've seen nothing yet. Because cloning is coming. And in our lifetimes too.

Booker-nominated Michael Collins related a story from his place of work, Microsoft in Seattle. One factor, claims Microsoft, that slows computers down is the English language. It's big, baggy, dirty, devious and adept at changing its spots. So why not give the software a break by reducing English to a necessary hardcore vocabulary?

The grave of George Orwell, I mentioned to Collins, is found in the English village of Sutton Courtenay. I had stood there a year previously, looking for something else, and found a white rose tree and a red rose tree hanging over the headstone. How their petals would fly as the writer revolved beneath. Collins shrugged. The woman who had that Newspeak brainwave was on the Microsoft fast-track. She would make her mark.

Collins is right, said a voice. In English. Stupidity is not the problem. The problem is intelligence. Intelligence has created more misery than stupidity ever could. Stupidity can be thwarted. But never intelligence. And what is intelligence doing now? Looking into the atom. And what does it see? That every atom has many rooms. And that those rooms are palaces too.

Don't worry. The more we see the more there will be to see. But truly the enemy is stupidity. The question is, how do we arm ourselves against it?

This sauna of debate was interrupted by evening readings. In Lahti's Sibelius Hall, an acoustics test proved the audience might hear a pin drop on stage. We bowed to the crowd in that resin-scented chancellery and toasted each other with Manohar Shetty's *feni*, an enamel-blistering Goan elixir distilled from cashew pulp.

The audience departed, switching its nokias back on, returning to the light that would not quit and plates of reindeer casserole. And to the trees. Because Finland is its trees. Without trees, it appeared to me, there could be no country called Finland at all.

I sympathised with the language irony. The irony that is always present at conferences such as Lahti. Here was I, an English language writer, representing a bilingual country that wasn't even a country, complaining about a shrinking world.

Easy for you to say, said the Byelorussians.

Easy for you to say, said the Lithuanians.

Typical of you to say, said the French.

To my aid I called Indian poet Manohar Shetty. But if Shetty writes in English, he remains multilingual. I quoted Nikolaj Stochholm, Danish poet now starting, slowly, to compose in English. But Stochholm is also, inevitably, a polyglot.

Thus it continued under Lahti's birchbark sky. It was the Russians who reminded us that if McDonald's was a clever stupidity, then the communism most Russians had experienced exemplified the malign variety. Which after a while became simply stupid stupidity. The kind of stupidity that gives stupidity a bad name.

A Russian joke was told to reveal what the Soviet system had done to personal initiative.

A woman notices two men at a roadside. The first man is

digging holes. The second man shovels the earth back in.

Woman: What are you doing?

1st Man: Planting trees.

Woman: No you're not. You're digging holes and that second man is filling them in.

2nd Man: I'm not the second man. I'm the third man. The second man didn't turn up.

Our definitions of stupidity heated up. A stupid society, said one delegate, was one founded on logic. Societies should be based on magic. But logic is the enemy of magic.

Another said that a stupid society is a sated society. Because real stupidity is stupefaction of the soul. Personally, I was hungover from the recent General Election in the UK. No wonder people refused to vote. They recognised stupidity when they saw it. Not a word about the global commons, climate change, drugs, the arts, the life of the mind. Instead, aridities about how the wealthy might become wealthier. Endless media interest in...nothing very much at all. It had dissipated so quickly.

I replayed the Russian joke. Or maybe it was an Albanian joke. It could have been a Welsh joke. But Welsh stupidity is of the abject variety. The new National Assembly – our infant parliament – has granted money for the destruction of the Dunlop factory domes at Brynmawr.

These had once comprised the largest spanned concrete structure in the world. The factory was a structural forerunner of the Sydney Opera House. The building was unique in the UK.

Now it is rubble. The demolition was financed by people who purport to have the vision to run a country. In truth, the Dunlop fiasco demonstrates failure of nerve and imagination at the highest political level. Stupidity and self-loathing demanded that the extraordinary be replaced with the anonymous. Abject indeed.

But who is the second man? The artist, surely. The Dunlop architect. The campaigner to save the domes. In

Wales, that 'country of employees' as a correspondent writes, the second man remains a rarity. So save the second man. We need the trees.

As these things do, our theme expanded to include the role of the writer in a stupid society. How should writers, even stupid writers, live? The writer has one duty, a delegate said. To live the writer's life. That is not a teacher's life. Neither is it an academic's life. And in case you are beginning to worry, he added, it is not an ascetic's life. *Skol*, he added, cupping a Koff.

A writer's life should be a life of the imagination. A life of thought and idea and impression. Then of learning how to put these into words. Then developing structures for such words. As simple as that. And if a writer has to teach it is not to teach the mechanics of poetry.

A poet who teaches poetry is a serpent swallowing its tail. The poet must convince the pupil that the imagination is a midnight sun. It never goes out. Then he must instruct the pupil how to read. Because reading dresses us. Reading feeds us. Reading warms us in a hostile climate. Without the life of the mind that reading provides we are naked and unnour-ished. Without the life of the mind we have no life at all. We are frail and impotent, at the mercy of fashion and politics and nationalism. *Etcetera*.

Was it night? Was it day? That titanium light might have brought dawn or dusk. For once, outside, the voices were stilled. The only sounds were the liturgies of the birch, the primaeval birch and spruce that have always covered this country.

Back in Helsinki, I roamed the city. It seemed deserted except for the poor and the very poor, the drunk and the very drunk. Everyone else had left for the lakes. For the trees. The nights were darker here, but stayed the colour of cigarette smoke. The only sounds were the wail of the Estonian ferry, the clinking of passing trams like a toast of vodka glasses.

Holed up downtown on Bulevardi with an enormous television, I watched MTV and BBC World. Eminem was the star of the former. Bad as I am, he raged. Bad as I am. Caged in computer music, he incited phoney hysteria. Behind the din he spat the rhymes. Yet his words seethed with a racked, if remote, intelligence.

Bad as it was, I've heard worse. BBC World, meanwhile, claimed it was volcanoes, not asteroids, that had done for the dinosaurs. And will do for us too, some day. Make no bones.

Then came a programme about Tirana. I was transfixed. How it has changed. Even the inhabitants cannot recognise it now. At home, I have framed a photograph of the tomb of Enver Hoxha. The grave of that absolutist bears a jamjar of weeds. When I visited Albania the first time it seemed a country from a fairytale. The people despaired under the enchantment of evil. Everything was broken.

And then, overnight, Ryan Giggs was ascending in a silver elevator. What was hot on the street were not samizdat poems or blackmarket loaves but Levi's and Nike ball caps. In the end, nothing could keep capitalism at bay. Not ignorance, not paranoia, not a million air-raid shelters. The invasion of Albania happened all right, but it came down the wire straight into the pleading soul.

From a great stupidity to a small stupidity. From stupid stupidity to clever stupidity. And hardly time between to look around and ask what kind of country Albania might have been. Or still might be.

Exhausted by the screen, I tried the bars. Leningrad Cowboys was closed, an unsprung bottle of Finlandia in every booth. Next was Erottaja. Wash out.

In U-Kaleva, spartan, local, I thought about where we had left the Lahti discussion on writers as teachers. There had been a woman standing behind me for some time. Now she stepped round, took the book I had balanced on my knee, kissed me.

Tickets? Passport? I never leave the country without my *New Directions* copy of Rimbaud's *Illuminations*. Prose poems and letters that serve as a philosophy. Especially the letters of May 1871, written when Rimbaud was sixteen. And a half. Coming up to his A levels, I suppose.

I cherish the book, disorientating, boundless, because it has often served as the antithesis to the world in which I grew up. "A prodigious and rational disordering of all the senses", the poet demands. Of himself and other poets. A *rational* disordering? Of *all* the senses?

No wonder we steer clear of the cracked kid these days. How easily he might offend the thin-skinned legions of the writing classes. Those letters are manifestos of scorn. But magnificent. The writer's attempt at decoding poetry's genome.

One thing Rimbaud does not do is endstop the imagination. And one thing he does is identify stupidity as the poet's enemy. So what would he make of my literalisms? Or of Lahti? And what would Rimbaud say to Eminem?

What problem? asked the woman.
I thought about it.
No problem, I said.
Her partner sneered at the next table. I noted his saurian eye. Unreconstructable pissheads. No question. The danger they radiated might have been my own unease.
I am lesbo, said the woman. She kissed me again.
I looked at the man. Days drunk. He sat slumped in a poisonous lethargy.
So am I, I said. And took Rimbaud from her like a baton.
Booze, I thought. Another thing that is really stupid. Really really stupid. The enemy of the writer. The enemy of the mind. Then I ordered another Koff medicine. Just to confuse myself.

Babble

I went to Babel once. There's not much left. The tower's gone, as you might have heard. Instead there's a crater with mud bricks at the base.

But there's a mosque. And when I was there, a pyramid of shoes. A big heap. It was prayer time and the men had taken off their shoes – sandals and trainers and some black Clark's. And all the men were inside the mosque. The mosque with the blue minarets.

But outside the mosque was a well. So I stood against a wall and looked at the boy, the waterboy, the servant of the well, and watched what he was doing. He seemed a happy child. Oh yes, he laughed a lot.

This boy put a stone in a bucket and lowered the bucket into the well and filled it and raised the rope and poured the Babel water into plastic bottles and jerry cans.

Then he did it again. And again. Women kept bringing him containers and he kept filling them up.

Yes, all the time I was watching, he did that. This laughing child. This boy pouring out the silver water – because it looked silver in the sun – and the drops he spilled darkening the dust around the well. The dust of Babel.

All that time I could hear the prayers from the mosque. Those voices like water, voices murmuring like the green Euphrates which was just over the hill, flowing there as it had always flowed.

And I thought, yes. There has always been a waterboy. Ever since Babel was built, there has been a waterboy, lowering a bucket, raising a bucket, weighting that bucket with a dark river pebble. A pebble from the Euphrates. A river-riven stone.

And I also thought, maybe God is in the well. Yes, maybe God is down there. Not in the mosque, not in our churches. But down there. In the well. Where the dark eye of water is the eye of God.

I thought that. Maybe an idle thought. Maybe a foolish thought. But then I thought something else. Maybe God is the well itself. And then I thought God might be the pebble. That river-riven stone.

Then I thought that God might be the bucket. The water? The well? The bucket? The pebble, that river-riven stone? Yes, leaning against a wall in Babel, those thoughts certainly crossed my mind.

Antares

(for Trevor)

A few years after it happened I started going to Beachy Head. High cliffs, white cliffs looking south. And I'd go in summer, really late on, because those June nights don't get properly dark until after midnight.

I'd go to see Antares. You know what that is? Antares is a star. A red star. In the constellation of the scorpion. Most times, I can't see it. Nobody can. It's too southerly, even from Beachy. But sometimes – yes, if I'm lucky, if it's a perfect night – Antares is there. So I just look. I sit on the grass, that bitten down grass on the chalk, and look out into the night. The night that's like the ocean.

Yes, as big as the ocean. And those June nights full of cockchafers. Big bugs, scary at first, but just clumsy. Flying around at the edge of things. Back and forth over the precipice and into thin air with the sea three hundred feet below. The sea milky with the chalk. So at night, it's a white sea.

Then low down, if I'm lucky, there's Antares. There it is. A dusky red like a pheasant's eye. Red as the dust of Morocco. A star red as chili oil. A glimpse of Berber gold.

And I think, Christ, I'm alive. Alive! Alive in all this, with these bugs divebombing and the sea a white mist, and the Milky Way a net in the sky, and the June night hardly a night at all. And a star like a ruby. Yes, a ruby in the navel of the night. Because I was sure I was done for. I was gone. *Finito*, I'm telling you. Over and out. I couldn't believe it.

When it happened everything seemed in slow motion. I could look down and see myself in the water. On the black swell. And my boat disappearing, with no-one on board who knew what had happened. Yes I looked down at myself – a man overboard, a man waving, a man calling. In the black swell.

And soon one red light on the stern was all I could see of that boat. That's all there was. The boat chugging away and me left behind, shouting, waving. That one red light on the horizon, down low. Not even a star can get any lower than that, I thought. But Antares can. I've learned that now. Because there it is, tonight. Antares on the southern horizon.

And then that red light vanished. Christ, I thought. I'm done for. This is it. Here I am on the shoulders of the swell. Thirty minutes is all I have. And the boat disappearing out of sight. Gone. Gone absolutely.

But what I'm trying to say is, that light vanishing was a good thing. Because it meant the boat was turning. The red star had vanished because the boat was coming back for me. Me on that big swell. In the white line of the wake, out in that immense clean blackness. No wave breaking. A world of black glass.

And I suddenly knew, yes, that they'd missed me. That the boat was turning. Because the star had vanished. Because the light was gone.

And that's why I come up here. To look out at the ocean and the sky, another ocean. And sometimes I see it and sometimes I don't. Antares, that is, the red star. The star of the stern.

I Know Another Way:
Walking To The Rhondda

"I know another way."

He would say that. Wouldn't he? The thin man.

I knew he was going to say that. The moment I'm sure of the route, north and north-west, past the Butcher's Arms in Llandaff, or off the cathedral green, along by the BBC, or maybe across to Whitchurch and the house called *Khasia*, north and north-west anyway, he has to offer his own alternative.

Which will involve roads not marked on any maps. Not that the thin man ever consulted a map, not in his own country. Those roads frost-heaved and rutted by the iron rims of hay-wagons and death-carts. Roads with burned-out Cavaliers on the corners but always an absence of traffic. Roads with pink armchairs abandoned under oak trees. Roads where buzzards wait like dismal pensioners for the bus that is a century too late. Roads that turn west when you're seeking the north. Roads that pass farms with ragwort in the *beilis*. Roads that are building sites with sycamores seeded in the foundations. Roads that double-back so you're surprised you don't meet yourself coming the other way. Roads under hedges black with bryony where a green cockscomb grows up the middle. Roads so narrow you must walk sideways. Roads to places that are no longer places. Roads to places only he would know.

Yes, he would say that, wouldn't he, the thin man, who is already leading me out of the suburbs, or the villages that became suburbs, good places, expensive places, all gnocchi and nokias now of course, but in their time part of a vision, a creed that honoured life. *I know another way*, he says. *But we can't start here.*

Yet start we must. Under the Llandaff Cathedral yews. I'm glad they're still here, alive and poisonous. Fifteen years ago I stood under these yews with a television journalist and local MP and talked about what acid rain was doing to the vitals of Wales. Frankly, I predicted doom. And was right. In a way.

Yet doom proves itself a cell by cell process. There was no apocalypse. So it's good to talk to the yews again, to acknowledge their reasonable health. Because the yew is a powerful tree. It comes out of the neolithic to us in an immemorial dynasty. Over its red dust we make our way, across to the Taff. We'll look at the river a while, then follow it north. The Taff's our compass needle. But the thin man needs no compass, he says. And we're travelling without the assistance of the Director General of the Ordnance Survey. What does he know and where has he been? So, not for the last time, let's stray a little.

The Taff in its time was a quilt of iron dust. It was a coal vein broken open to the light. The Taff was once so thick with coal, people claimed its waters looked like funeral crepe. But now the final indignity. They have taken away its tides.

Because the Taff drowns itself in the teaspoon of the Cardiff Barrage. Back there at Llandaff and now at Taff's Well it flows beside me, coming out of the carboniferous. It pushes through the circlet of limestone that rings the coalfield of south Wales on the geological map. That coalfield is coloured grey as a tumour, though as a Cardiff poet has told us, tumours might ripen into mauve.

So here it runs. Silver, suicidal. It has otters and trolleys and toilet paper, kingfishers and colliers on its conscience. And of children like poor Wiffin, there's no counting.

At the same time as in Taff's Well it is behind us at

Llandaff. There in the cathedral, Epstein's Christ is squeezing himself out of an enormous toothpaste tube. Simultaneously the river is flowing through Bute Park and into the city's aboretum, and surely of the cities I know it's only Rio has a richer rainforest in its midst. On to our glass parliament it runs, and the Millennium Centre. So let's hear it for the Taff. Let's drown its own aria with an oratorio of our own, then allow the First Minister to offer a valediction as the river slumps into the dock beside him, *Guilty, your Honour, Guilty as Sin*, and its name is dissolved in the Bay's acid bath.

I'm walking north. But in less than a mile the way is blocked. Here's the motorway – a Serengeti for the age of speed. I stand on the M4 bridge below Radyr watching its metronome of life. And such life, a teeming ecology, the prey and the predatory mixed in together.

Usually, where there's no going over, I go under. Under at Kenfig to the sand-scoured castle. Under at Llewellyn Street where you might lean from the terrace windows and touch the concrete piles. Under at The Cymdda where the new Wales has been constructed overnight in the ultra violet of the Odeon and the sacristy of McArthur Glen. And when you stand under the motorway and read the writing on its pillars, when you hear the unrelenting wheels above your head, you know the motorway for what it is: a path of pilgrimage.

Because we all commute. The sea twice a day, the call centre Kayleighs, the DIY warehouse Garins, the planets in rare affiliation in the north west tonight, which is the direction we're taking. Commuters are the pilgrims today and if there's anything I've learned it's that we are pilgrims or we are nothing. There's white van man in the fast lane, that pilot fish of commerce, because if ever there was a pilgrim it is white van man, gunning it to destiny, 90, 95, the orgasmic ton.

And there stalled on the hard shoulder, the saleswoman's Focus. And you and I in the hayrattle meadow that is now the Grenada forecourt at Cardiff West. Ten minutes later we can be above The Cymdda where one day the cottongrass and peatwater black as espresso will be restored. Because this is it: our Great Barrier Reef. And there's no better place to observe it than this bridge. I suppose I could have dashed across, there are gaps in the traffic. Yet only the bridge permits this panorama. And what a place to stand. This is our balcony in the eye of the storm as the M4 disappears in its ribbon of platinum dust and the cherry blossom streams into the drains.

With me on the road through Gwaelod y Garth is Edward Lhuyd. We stopped at the pub, although the village hostelry considers itself an inn, and indisputably an inn it is, a stone tavern built from the stone that rises behind it and gives the village its name and purchase. But only for a couple, though already my legs are as heavy as my head is light, and now on the road through the fields our talk is of garlic.

My attention at the bar had been drawn by a young woman with a bowl of soup. How she sipped, gracefully as an avocet, her upturned spoon its upturned beak, over the gleaming mere. But Lhuyd had been arrested by garlic twiglets. By garlic mayonnaise. By the garlic-flavoured crisps, the scree and swarf scented with garlic in their sealed purses, the iron filings flavoured with garlic in saucers upon the counter, the limestone chews impregnated with garlic, the granite shavings immersed in garlic, the beechwood toast and oaken baguettes overwhelmed by garlic.

I had enjoyed our snack, but Lhuyd's teeth are not what they were. I try to stop his complaint. After all, there are bullfinches in the hedge, their breasts so red you'd think them naked, there are buzzards catcalling over the wood, and yes, Lhuyd is right, there is a white road of garlic that follows our road, that bends when it bends, that climbs as we rise.

There's no time to stop so we taste as we go. Certainly Lhuyd is right. This is garlic as it should be, this is garlic with the rain on it, wild garlic under its white veil, a wedding trail of garlic in the grass behind us, and here's the ghost of garlic on my fingers, a succulence that won't let go.

Common enough, I say, chewing another leaf.

"*Allium ursinum,*" he says.

"Ramsons," I say. "Or is it ransoms. Ransoms is better. As in the poem. Sort of a wild onion. Long may it hold me to ransom."

"Of the family *Liliaceae.*"

"Well answer me this," I say. "Why did we never cook with it? Here it is, free food. A larder a mile long. And no recipes for wild garlic. Not poisonous, is it"?

"Pigs wouldn't eat it"

"Think," I say. "We could have put in soups. In stews. Cooked our meats with it. All that tough mutton. All that bad cheese. It's crying out for ransoms. All that bread that smells like library books".

"Horses wouldn't look at it."

"We could sell it," I say. "We could bag it up and sell it in Ponty market for a quid a bunch. Make us rich."

Lhuyd goes quiet. The light, as we climb, devastates. The view grows with every step. But we see only as far as we allow ourselves. There are so many greens you'd need a National Gallery of Green to reproduce them.

"What's that?" I ask, pointing. There's another white flower following us. It's been there a long time. No matter how fast we walk, we can't throw it off.

"Ah", says Lhuyd. "*Stellaria holostea.* Shirtbutton. In your language, the greater stitchwort. Adder's meat."

"So we can eat it"?

Lhuyd says nothing.

Eventually we stop at the entrance to a wood. He tells me that the wood is filling like a butt of rainwater almost to the brim. He talks of enchanter's nightshade. He describes dog's mercury. He points to the twaybladed orchid with its undistinguished spire. We walk on. There are bluebells under the sycamores in a reef that stretches as far as I can see.

"On your knees," says the botanist.

On our knees we breathe the scent. But I prefer looking.

Yet looking is dangerous.

There is something hallucinatory about bluebells. As I gaze at these flowers I suspect a narcotic in the air. Such is their perfume, such is the quality of their blue. I am underwater now and the blue's a balm somehow inside my eyes and I am swimming in its lagoon. Surely these flowers are poisonous. Because soon I'm paralysed.

But my mind is walking on, though beside me Lhuyd lies down. This is as far as he goes, he says, for this wood is a bower quiet for us, and a sleep full of sweet dreams, and health, and quiet breathing.

It's not long before I reach Taff's Well. The village is engulfed by roads. Here's Omega Security, its dogs, its cameras, so many cameras on this route we might make a CCTV movie of ourselves stumbling out of the woods and into the revolution of consumer paranoia.

I've been a trespasser all my life, and pilgrim, you should be aware of that if you're following this trail. Under the barbed wire, away from the beaten track; watching for farmers on Suzukis, gamekeepers in Taff-coloured corduroy. Once it was child's play to leave their prosecuting voices behind. But they are the old enemy. It's a new game now and there's less of a future in trespassing as the cameras turn like flowers towards the sun and reveal who stirs in the stonewashed small hours.

Yet something is barring the way. I've arrived at the heart-breaking sheds of the supermarket, so large they might hold aeroplanes. But this is no factory, and in I go under the cameras that caress all that enter, and at once with who knows what atavistic instinct, I find I've adopted the sleepwalkers' demeanour necessary to prove myself a supplicant of the store.

Half a mile away is Castell Coch. Which is where you might be now, rapping on the portcullis, imagining Lady Bute stepping out of her chemise as she looks down at the treetops from her bedchamber. But if you've followed me you'll see

I'm pricing Leeward Island bananas, figs from Greece. Then energy drinks that Fed-ex caffeine to the blood; proteins that restore hope, vitamins that recover determination.

I'm down one aisle and up the next, eyes left, eyes right. We need it all, we need the world, its sunflower seeds rattling in my basket, the staff of fair trade chocolate to help me over what's to come. Now I'm searching for something to feed the imagination. Starfruit? Peccarino or paracetamol? Maybe pumpernickel, wheatgerm, or the phials of the detox shelves. Or lollo rosso, groundnuts, evening primrose. What about enchiladas, gewurztraminer, zinfandel? Perhaps chili dog, happy dog, slush, crush, the original Neapolitan peasant recipe with extra cheese? Because we're all ravenous in the land of plenty, lost in the supermarket's garden of forking paths.

It's not Castell Coch. But we might as well enjoy it. The place is big as a small town. At every hour it boasts such a town's population. This is a high street under striplights and people are here because other people are here and there's gossip and glamour and only for the dwindling few the memory of what existed before it was built, the voices under the ground: the shiggling lamps, the blackpats.

Soon, life before the supermarket will be an inconceivable past. And then, when it is sufficiently strange, when it is irrecoverable, we will make films about it and statues will be raised and historians will give judgement and the rest of us will shrug and think there but for the grace of God goes... but Lady Bute at the checkout is asking if I need cashback. Look, pilgrim, here's a miracle indeed. I'm leaving with fifty more than when I came in. Happy dog.

Immediately I stand in a predicament of roads. The straightest route is around Taff's Well and north on the minor road between ash trees whose black buds have yet to unfurl and more of those shirtbuttons rolling in the grass.

This week I met the poet, Landeg White, who left Taff's Well aged five and has not returned. Until now. I am reading his book, *Traveller's Palm*, which reeks of his time in Africa, of its maize porridge and prison cells, and of his Portuguese home with its carafes of green wine. No-one in Taff's Well remembers Landeg White. No-one in Wales remembers him. The poet made the mistake of becoming exotic. But now the son has returned. Ah well, I shrug, and turn aside from the road.

Instead I retreat towards The Garth. Up, over, and here is Efail Isaf and not a soul to be seen in the village. In a garden I watch a sparrowhawk alight. It seizes a young blackbird. Soon around the hawk is a circle of feathers. Outside that circle is a circle of silence where nothing can intrude. Outside that second circle is a circle of uncertain silence. And outside that circle is the grief of the cock bird's voice. It approaches the hawk as closely as it dares. But the two circles of silence are forbidden to it. It watches as its chick is torn apart and devoured. Then the hawk rises and takes a second bird. Looking around the lawn, it makes the killing with its spur, calm at the centre of the circles where the rite is performed. Soon there are two circles of feathers, each with two circles of silence around them. The world is forbidden to enter those circles. The blackbird is forbidden and I know I am forbidden. No creature, no magic or sacrifice can alter the power of those circles. They were drawn before we discovered the purpose of our minds.

When the hawk flies off the circles disappear and soon there's cuckoo spit on my legs and the pennants of lords-and-ladies beginning to thrust aside the litter, snake berries we used to call them, and here's a field full of milkmaids close to white-painted St. Illtud's at Upper Church Village and you might look a long time for milkmaids in the dictionaries and come away disappointed, but this is my childhood around me, smoking out of the dew, pollen poltergeists moving ahead and behind, and I can put a face and a name to every one of those ghosts, for these are my traveller's palms and at this instant it seems impossible to believe that anything lost will not eventually be returned.

Footsore, I'm in the lanes. There's a whirlpool of trails around here. I know a better way, said the thin man, but we're going west when I know east of Mynydd y Glyn is called for. There are S bends and empty road signs and if this is the way to Pontypridd it is the route I would take in a post-apocalpyse Wales when all former identities have vanished and there's no right and no wrong.

Here at a crossroads is another hollow sign, and tied to barbed wire is a cellophane bouquet. Someone must have died in this place. Somebody lost or travelling too fast, eager to leave this country that has no name. What should be happening now is our descent into Graig, dangerous for pedestrians, and our triumphant arrival in Taff Street.

But I travel with a companion who thinks he knows a better way and soon there's a notice on a wall that confirms my suspicions. 'Pant y Brad' it says. Even I know that '*brad*' means treachery, and if you've been fool enough to follow us you will have already understood that something underhand is going on. Because if this is Pant y Brad we have come south-west of the Rhondda Fawr.

If this is Pant y Brad I've betrayed my own instincts. It means our road now must lead to Tonyrefail, dreary Ton that must have something going for it, and, be my guest, traveller, discover what's hidden here. Then up to Trebanog and the man with a pitbull guarding the entrance to the Rhondda. Cerebus is straining at both leash and belly-belt and its handler follows with his own pitbull's gait, the dog wheezing, the man in a white singlet pulling it back into the Rhiwgarn estates where I consider it unnecessary to follow, Rhiwgarn being Rhiwgarn.

Not that Taff Street's Easy Street. In its day it knew tumultuous trade. Maybe there are reminders of that past for those who know where to look. But the Queen of the Valleys is on librium now, and as you see, here's more *brad*.

I've doubled back, gone down the Graig. To find myself

peering into the window of Mid Glamorgan Goldsmiths. Who must be pleased with themselves. Young Ponty men have adopted the fashions of The Bronx and East New York. They drip with chains and bracelets, their knuckles are fat with signet rings as they reach for their phones. See them best on the Friday night parade between the Market Tavern and Angharad's. Here are the Ponty girls too, in clingy gangs, crop-topped and pale-bellied. Shivering like eels come out of the stream.

The town looks exactly what it is. A place from which certainty has ebbed. The traditional life choices have vanished: men in the pit, the women at home or stitching underwear in The Rhondda, and on a Saturday night a visit to the Town Hall for 'Billy Maxman the Wonder Fool' followed by 'Yeaman's Famous Footballing Dogs'.

Yet maybe that's naive. Pontypridd was always the most middle class of valley towns. I used to teach evening classes at Coed y Lan and remember substantial villas with evergreen gardens overlooking the terraces. And there has always been money and elegance as well as radical politics in Graigwen.

But Queen of the Valleys? It's a republican age. What Ponty cries out for is exploration of its teeming history and problematical present by artists and writers. No town deserves it more. Alun Richards is Ponty's most famous literary son, while John L. Hughes's angry *Tom Jones Slept Here* is worth searching for in second-hand book shops. If any now exist.

Yet what we need is an urban lyricist with a pathologist's eye (but not a pathologist's mind); a bedsitter scientist who can interpret the genome of contemporary English. And if that sounds romantic, all well and good. Real writers are always romantics but rarely admit to it. Because to write today in Pontypridd is an exhilarating romantic act.

As to anger, choose it, use it, but get over it. Anger was never the most innovative search-engine of the writer's imagination.

Pilgrims grow thirsty. By chance, here is the Trehafod Hotel. It's ten years since I stood in the public bar and I'm trying to understand what's changed. Nothing, it seems. Nothing apart from everything. Because I'm a new man. Since I last stood here every cell in my body has died and been reborn. The carbon is new, the hydrogen new. Like those Hopkinstown homies I'm priceless with new gold.

Maybe minds too are reborn. Perhaps there is a renaissance of the imagination. Then why does the spirit fail? Why do we give up the ghost if the ghost too is a new ghost? Before me the atoms of the mirror are dead atoms. The uptipped double litre of London Dry with its juniper garland will never undergo rebirth. And there are my greyed hairs in that mirror that were never there before, while my thoughts conspiring now around the gin were not previously concerned with time.

Time? It's massing around me like Mynydd y Glyn, there to the west. It's building itself in the east like The Glôg. And squeezing me into it. Another fossil in its cliff. Now The Glôg I can stand. And maybe Mynydd y Glyn I might negotiate. But I know what's coming. Cefn Craig Amos, that's what's coming. Pilgrim, that's a brutal ridge. There'll be no shrugging off Cefn Craig Amos, no optimism about scaling that precipice.

But that's the future. That's the end of this journey. And what's ten years? A moment. So make your tribute to the god of thirst here in the Trehafod Hotel. And think of the moments of which The Glôg is built.

The pilgrimage progresses even as we rest. And soon you will notice that the Trehafod Hotel is no place for the pious. There are pieties here innumerable, but the pious should beware. And now it arrives. Your drink. The drink you have ordered but which in another reality has been ordered for you. It's been waiting a long time.

There is always something numinous about a pint come over the bar. Forget what it costs and ignore its antecedence. It will taste like the Taff yet reassemble your perceptions of self. It will instil holiness before the paranoia starts, but life is impossible without the delusions your glass will bring to you.

In Llandaff in the Butcher's you might sit under the Brain's diamond in your own blue diamond of smoke and know that the path taken is no more crooked than the path to come. In Graigwen at the Ty Mawr the regulars will know you for a pilgrim before you have carried your glass to your seat and they will understand entirely that pilgrimage but not easily illustrate their understanding. And at The Rickyard Arms coming down the hill towards Porth and its bazaar, selling Queen Elizabeth Jubilee street party union jacks (discount), we might stand Gwyn Thomas a drink. But choose a seat near the door. Exits are important to Gwyn.

Less garrulous than of old, he has his opinions.

"What's become of the Rhondda, Gwyn"?

"What indeed?"

"Who are these inheritors, Gwyn, in their NY ballcaps and Adidas training gear? In their white trainers with shock absorbers in the toes? No steelies now, Gwyn. Their feet are soft."

"NY?" he asks. "Ah yes. *Not Yours.*"

"So who are these Rhondda men, Gwyn, heads shaved, faces ringed and pierced?"

"The sons of their fathers", the maestro breathes, over his American cream soda. "No more, no less. But don't ask me what they do. Work has changed".

And he thinks a moment. "Do people work these days? I know they're busy. Sometimes I watch the boys when their phones ring. That instant of bliss. Somebody's calling. Somebody cares. And there's me," he says, taking a first sip, "who hasn't had a telephone call since 1981."

"Mr Thomas," I say. "Tell me one thing before you go. I've always wanted to know why people planted monkey puzzle trees in the Rhondda?"

"Ah! Our great conundrum," he says. "I've counted them all. And each is a friend. A little misplaced, aren't they, but brave. It's their bravery I admire. And the pretention too. Which is always one thing we lacked. Pretention. How we were warned against it. That was our great virtue, see. Our unpretentiousness. But sometimes people make vices out of their virtues..."

And then he has to borrow a handkerchief because the cream soda bubbles have gone up his nose.

But as in The Rickyard, two miles closer to where we are heading today, or two miles further away, as Mr Thomas put it before slipping out, here in the Trehafod a word of advice. Be wary of the landlord's expression. Vacancy and animation are masks. Both angels and demons are found behind public-house counters and I have been obliged by both. The deranged inhabit these places. The deranged are people who do not share your derangement. The stupid too are found in here. The stupid are those who do not acknowledge your wisdom. There will be cowards also, who will not credit your courage.

Above all, admit the ritual. The nun with her Bristol Cream, the murderer with his low-cal, have sat where you sit now. Under the window in a torrent of spring light. Thirst is our dangerous blessing. It is as if our glasses were a pilgrim-age's reward and the pilgrim's absolution.

So, drink up. But know that glass for either a piety or an enchantment. They are similar conditions. Which is something you should not ponder too long at the Trehafod Hotel.

We're now either ahead of ourselves or behind. But don't worry. We're all going to the same place. And Trehafod is instructional for those attuned to the lessons of history. Here's what's left of Lewis Merthyr colliery, but unlike the hundreds of other coal mines in the valley, it has not been grassed over or turned into a superstore. It's now the site of the Rhondda Heritage Park, dedicated to mining.

A brief visit will confirm two suspicions. First, winning coal was a terrible trade. Second, existentialism never made it to the coalfield. The miners were heroes, but obedient heroes, as their wives were heroic and obedient in their turn. And together, men and women mined the inexhaustible seam of their own loyalty. Even as the walls collapsed, even as their children were scalded to death or were wasted by rickets and diphtheria, even as the money haemorrhaged south into the starry boudoirs of Castell Coch and on to the Mount Stuart banks where the world's first cheque for a million pounds was penned, they remained paragons of obedience. Instructional, traveller? Oh yes, at Trehafod we might learn a good deal about ourselves.

But whose heritage is this? Mine, indubitably. Who was never down a pit. In his life. Who will always refuse any invitation to the memorial shafts. So at Trehafod I visit the fan engine house.

Of all colliery equipment, the fan engine was the most important. Here, I think of the draughts the engines blew underground and imagine those purifying blasts travelling through darkness on the way to the lungs of the thousands who cut the coal and filled the drams. Of fresh air invading the colonnades and the dead ends, its incense chilling the skin; fresh air from the censors of the fan engines blowing down the coal roads. Fresh air lengthening the sentences of those already condemned.

There's no amnesia at Trehafod. But even here, or especially here, when I try to think of the coalfield, that tumour intrudes. The tumour on the map. Maybe I was a fool to hang it on my wall, that map of an unpeopled Wales, the map of the arbitrary grains beneath our feet: a free Wales indeed of mudstone and volcanoes and the physics of rock, a pre-Cambrian Wales, a pre-Wales Wales.

I pass them every day, those western peninsulas with their psychedelic geology, on my commute from study to kitchen. Then there is the limestone of north and south, and a pagan rainbow in the east: the witch country around Church Stretton. And last the coalfield painted in grey and etched with a forest of faults.

The pits are closed but coal cannot be escaped. I walk on the southern beaches every afternoon and find coal mingled with the sand. There's a seam that runs a mile under the sea near where I live. The old Newlands pit was worked for decades, so clean was that coal, the miners curling themselves like trilobites into the seabed, taking light and language and their own hot blood into places where they didn't belong, into places where no life belongs unless it is blind and cold and unnameable.

And on those beaches I hear the fairground, the cries from the SkyMaster, the Ghost Train, and yes, the coalfield will always be a ghost train to me, a ghost train shuttered for the night and the winter, but where as if in a dream I am leased to wander through its corridors, passing the faces of legend in their shrines, the dead and the undead, the eyes, the mouths, the victims, the victorious, all fossils together in those dungeons, and every passage indistinguishable from the last.

If it's a labyrinth there is only one guide who can take us through. Because if the coalfield is a labyrinth only Jorge Luis Borges knows the way out. Yes, maybe that's how I see the coalfield now. A labyrinth with a dead minotaur. A labyrinthine library whose books are fossils. A library of Babel where everything is written but nothing is read.

Yes, let Borges take us through, and let us search with him for the last miner, the lost miner whom only Borges can find in these circular ruins, because only a Borges can bring back our Taff Steet Theseus who has let go the thread, but who still clutches his snap, his lamp, his vocabulary of extinct trades, and who hews at the rock every day beneath our feet.

"Could have come in from there," gestures the thin man, waving at the east and the Rhondda Fach. "Over the mountains from Llanwonno."

I know the road. It comes through a forest, melancholy at the best of times. But it's drama he describes. Because there's drama at every entry to these valleys. You have to fight to get into the Rhondda. You have to want to be there. Whether it's over Bwlch y Clawdd to the west, the Rhigos and Llethr Las to the north, or scowling Trebanog where the mastiff lurks, it's what a pilgrimage should be.

I know another way, said the thin man, and now we're looking down over the momentous vale. There are the roofs of the Rhondda Fawr, and when we turn there is the waste tip that is coal's sarcophagous, the colour and shape of Silbury Hill.

"I used to know its name," he says. In this light there's a sinister geometry to the tip. I shake my head.

We had come through Wattstown and Ynyshir, then taken the hill. Now on Penrhys we stare and listen to the dogs. There's no chance of refreshment. At the top of the estate we call at the Pendyrus RAOB Social Club but the doors are barred. Above us are the conifers but this is as high as we get. A burned out bus shelter. The blackened satellite dishes hanging like wreaths.

There's a cry in Heol Teifionydd, a whisper in Heol Pendyrus. And then a silence. Somehow here we are out of the world. We passed a boundary somewhere or blundered through a forcefield and now stand beyond what's familiar. Children are playing in a puddle, there's washing on the lines, but it's clear we've crossed a frontier. It's a different world and I don't belong. Traveller, may it be otherwise for you.

All I know is that Penrhys was designed like a village overlooking the Tyrrhenian sea. Yet often the wind that blows here feels as if it has crossed Iceland. And that when the locals stare at me I cannot meet their eyes. Yes this is as high as I will ever reach above the Virgin on her lawn.

I look at the statue. It's a glum and bone-coloured Mary we find, this virgin of the oaks. Nearby are ruined chapel walls where once the medieval poor came to worship. Visitors should bring their own exultancy to this place. They will find little here. If their Welsh is good enough, they'll learn that the original statue was destroyed – *dinistriwyd* – such an emphatic word – on September 26, 1538. This replacement was erected in 1953. A little nun from Porthcawl, brown as a fieldfare, was one of those who suggested the restoration of the shrine. She took a party of schoolgirls up the windy hill. One of the pupils walked with a leg-iron. The other girls waited for the miracle.

John Newman in his *Buildings of Glamorgan* wrote that the statue would seem to belong "in Ecuador". With which we should all disagree. Exquisite it is not, but its creators should be allowed their bold design. How well we've been trained to ridicule the pretentious. *Remember the monkey puzzle,* hisses a ghost.

We're finished here. And begin again. I leave the valley by another way, the road north into Ferndale and on to Maerdy. Poor Maerdy. Little Moscow they used to call it. But now they don't call it very much at all, this part of the Rhondda Fach being somewhat on its uppers, and there's North Terrace which is where the Rhondda ends, and there is Institute Street where its ghost laments.

Because here is the sad baroque of the Institute itself, one of the great remaining buildings of this world, a library, a theatre, and a statement made by workers' pennies if ever such a statement was made, and if you come this way remember it was the thin man who suggested it, and note the lesson of Pant y Brad. Yet if you still decide to take this road, push open the Institute's metal doors and step inside. Then gaze at what remains of generations of self-sacrifice.

This will happen under the shadow of Cefn Craig Amos. I promised you that ridge and here it is: a bulwark that hides the sun and chills the waters of the Rhondda Fach. There's a school built in its shadow. No place for a school, I think, looking at the unremitting rock, thinking of the classrooms dark in the morning and those cliffs shuttering their glass. But already we are leaving it behind. We're going beyond.

Because what are any of us if not pilgrims? For me, at least, that's an attractive thought. An explanatory thought. It clarifies a good deal about my life. Whether in the museum or Gwaelod's limestone maw or the slumland shrine of Penrhys, all of us pursue a sacred commute: white van-man, Kayleigh from the Call Centre, and the crachach of the Beeb breathing into their Samsungs. Yes, even Pontcanna will know its Pentecost.

And remember that the Taff, first pilgrim to be encountered in the hereabouts of this essay, on the way to an ignominious end, must begin somewhere out of our reckoning. In a droplet no bigger than a grain of rice.

The Sunflower

In the coffin lay Santa Margherita. A holy ape. She was green as an olive. So this was what death did, reducing the body to earth, but an earth without rainshine or windflash.

The pious too craned to see. For them the seven hundred year survival of the body of Saint Margaret is a miracle. But there was nothing for me in that church. So I climbed further, as far as the town allowed.

At the top was the Fortezza di Gyrfalcon which had become an art gallery. Through the window I watched a hawk, not the gyrfalcon yet a thrilling predator. As it swept the hill its wings gleamed like willow leaves, bronze and silver, light and dark. Over the plain the view stretched into immensities.

I had been following the poet John Ormond around Cortona, the impossibly-positioned Tuscan town he had come to love. Ormond adopted Cortona as a spiritual home, the place where he felt most true to himself.

I had with me the hardback (only) edition of *Requiem and Celebration*, published by Christopher Davies in 1969 when the writer was 46. This is a book worth considering, not least for its sleeve notes by Glyn Jones. These constitute a critical essay and are a world and a culture removed from the hyperbole that disfigures so many new volumes of poetry. Because an editor these days must exist in a state of slight but permanent nausea, surrounded as s/he is by the hagiography concocted by publishers, agents and the writers themselves.

Beyond Cortona stretched fields of sunflowers. These sunflowers had died. Each one was tall as a scarecrow, every

face a black zodiac. But their seeds were sharp in their
satchels. Sunflowers must die of course, but not uniformly.
And surely these sunflowers were for harvesting. Maybe they
had been gassed. How like an army they paraded in their
phalanxes. An army bowed in defeat.

John Ormond has no new readers. His public is a wilting
band. I know this because Ormond's *Selected Poems* is techni-
cally available from Seren. But no more than a handful of
copies exist. Until there is public or academic pressure no
Collected will appear. This is an irony because it was writers
such as Ormond whose examples created the literary world
we have today: apolitical, and founded on a private vision
dependent upon global reference. John Ormond's role model
in this was Dylan Thomas, whose life suggested that the artist
could combine happy-go-lucky rootlessness with intimate
belonging.

Yet John Ormond also had a career as a BBC film maker.
Typically, his best work features other poets. However, his
admiration for their achievements led him to doubt his own
powers – to engender what Glyn Jones describes as "dissatis-
faction", Ormond's career exhibiting "an unrelenting
struggle to find his own true subject-matter".

Or maybe the sunflowers had been poisoned. Sunflowers
must die but I find their deaths grievous. On my allotment
under the church of St John the Baptist in Porthcawl, the
sunflowers were vigorous last year. One day in September I
climbed the entrance stile and there lay a ten foot specimen,
its stem a mast, its face a pub-sign, the whole apparatus
ridiculous as a broken speak-your-weight machine. But by
late October a grove of sunflowers still survived the wester-
lies. Black and thistley, they hummed like a substation, faces
glum as rusted Sky TV dishes.

When I lived on my own in Saskatchewan I used to talk to
a sunflower. It grew in the garden and nodded from its bench
like some green-wigged JP. As Fall progressed it declined,
shrivelling with sunflower osteoporosis, its seeds ripped out

by buff-coloured waxwings. Yet this sunflower seemed to retain its wisdom. Then the first night of real cold reduced it to a saint in a glass casket. By the second it was an X-ray of itself. That was how sunflowers were supposed to die. With dignity. But the Cortona sunflowers seemed snuffed out overnight in shameful conformism.

To find John Ormond's 'Note from Cortona' readers will have to track down that elusive *Selected Poems*. Thus they might learn how and why Italy inspired such a niggardly poet. Yet the pity of it is that younger writers have almost no access to the bulk of his writing.

What we need is a film maker of Ormond's precision to create a biography of the man and the artist. For that 'dissatisfaction' is the antidote to what can appear to an editor as the cynical promotion of mediocrity. Because in John Ormond writers today might find a role model. And that is of no mean significance.

Being a Description of Those I Encountered during my Sojourn on the Island of Lightning

1. A Catalogue of Ships

Increasingly I seek out Omar because he knows things. In fact Omar seems to understand most that happens on the island.

Because the city is an island. I've proved that to myself in my increasingly ambitious expeditions. But Omar also understands what has already happened, and I'm sure that's the key. That's the secret to this place. And that's the secret that interests me. Because the past will explain the gods. The gods of this island.

One day I join the party of Germans Omar is leading around the ramparts. With two blonde fraus in leather and mimosa I have my photograph taken beside a cannon. The barrel points out to sea, the cannon balls are piled in a pyramid at our feet. Black seed, I think. The iron hearts of the papaya fruit.

There's a cat, one of the island's orange cats, curled on the cannon balls. All the cats here, so my scouting tells me, belong to one clan; the skinny, manky, orange clan. And how they love the sun. Even this scabby tom is sleek in its beam.

After thanking their guide, the party drifts away. I join Omar at a table in Café Leone and we talk about the weather. How unseasonably warm it is. I want to ask Omar about the gods, but he seems determined that I should learn about the island's ships and the captains of those ships.

Yes, says Omar. Our fortune is built on such men. So God

help us. First there's Oscar, who lives in a hovel on Mediterranean Street. Oscar's family have been sailors since the beginning. But Oscar likes the marsovin too much. He owns a paint-bleached barkazza and a broken gondola, and he sails out of an evening, looking for octopus.

Then there's Georgiou of St. Ursula Street, who steals lobsters from the pots under the western ramparts. That used to be a capital offence, I've seen men keelhauled for such. But of course, a sailor is a man and a man must live. So don't mind Georgiou. His barque is worse than his bight.

Have you met Manoel from Eagle Street? Ah, Manoel, he braves seas so rough in that old ketch of his, you think he's never coming back. Force nine is a child's breath to Manoel. But as I say, fishermen must live and Manoel casts nets for bristling and white pilchard.

And you must have seen the African from the warren in the walls? He's made a boat from the planks of other boats, bits of driftwood and floats. He sets off in that raft with his five-tanged fork searching for angel shark. Maybe he was a great captain in his own country, which is Sierra Leone, a kingdom of cruelties where most of the murderers are children. Or so I'm told. And yes, there are scars on his back, healed violet. And burns on his wrists and ankles. But sometimes I look at him and see a stateliness in his eye.

Then there's Hilario of South Street who puts to sea in a gharbiel, the water coming through the joints, a real sieve, hardly a bucket, more like a nightsoil barrel, yes a pisspot with a crack in it, that's Hilario's galleon, mad old Hilario who couldn't catch himself but one morning came back with a mermaid, and friend I tell you, Hilario married this mermaid and she lived with him on South Street. Well, that's the story. Dispute it with Hilario when he's sober. He comes out with us sometimes when we go after flapperskate. Bloody old Hilario, he's fathomless to me, bobbing out there like a cork, an old man astride his mustardiera, the wind taking the sail of his trousers. Old Hilario, blown along by his farts.

Of course you can't forget Marcello, coming across the harbour in his scutch. That's Marcello of St. Elmo Street where there are more boats than headlice and the nets hang like spiderwebs.

Now Michelangelo, he lives on Old Theatre Street and works on the dredger, 'Sapphire' in the grand harbour. He borrows his brother's gondola and rows to the islet where the softbodied crabs live in the rock pools. Sometimes he brings us a coffeesack full, the whole bag wriggling and the crabs wheezing like tiny bellows. That's a peculiar music to hear at dawn.

Don't forget McCale, the nostromomu. He doesn't usually come on our voyages. But he offers us stories. Once, marooned on the Black Isle, he milked a cowfish. That's how he survived. The milk, he said, tasted as diamonds might taste, though salty as caviar. Yes, yes, McCale we say, go back to your cactus juice and Neptune save the ships you steer towards port. Why not sleep it all off in St. Pawlu Street with your fat wife?

Then there's Aurelio, a good boy from the poorest barrakka on the western side, who will dive from the side of any boat and bring back cowries. Once he came up with an oyster filled with a rainwater-coloured pearlseed that somehow Hilario swallowed when he was sniffing it. May it grow to choke that imbecile. Or maybe I think, maybe Hilario is not as stupid as he pretends. That gumboil of his…

Of course, there's the Macedonian too. He cannot swim nor sail and once went round all night under the moon. We found him the next morning in the same place and that Macedonian moonstruck, babbling away in his abominable Greek. We gave him espressos in the QE2 bar, and the next day he brought us aubergines from his garden, and sweet peppers he had grown in a window box. Stay home we told him, and water your seeds, or we will be lighting a candle in a red glass for you down at the shipwreck church. The fool had seen meteors all night and had thought them portents of his own death. Ah, we laughed there in the tavern, you must be a great man for heaven to fill with fire for you. Look, we'll take you to the fishmonger in the suq so you can learn why we sail out. Why we do what we do. But no more ragtime with ragworm for you.

Maybe you've seen Azzopardi, who weights his line with a sparkplug and casts for flounder from the stern of the pilot boat when there's no traffic in the bay. You never know what's there in all that oil and plastic, he says, in all the shit from the Russian billionaire's yacht and all the cruise liners with the captains in gold braid and the retired bank managers in their white tuxedos looking down at the greasy dock. I spit on them. Hey Azzo, we say, watch they don't spit on you. You'll never see it coming. But who knows what lives in the port. A child brought a sea horse once, nodding in a pickled onion jar. And once there was a harbour dolphin laughing as if it had heard the greatest joke in the world. Old Azzo lives in the apartments on Saint Guseppi Street, but his salmon is John West and then only on Friday. Hey presto, Azzo we shout, are you coming? And he comes.

Sometimes we have Ahmed too, from East Street, who will light a candle at Our Lady of Damascus before every voyage, because, my friend, even our pleasant excursions are voyages. For those in peril on the sea? Please don't smile. We are seafarers too.

But Ahmed we say, you have no place in a good Catholic church. Go and bow your head and wiggle your arse under your broken moon. And Ahmed calls us ignorant fools for not knowing our history, and I agree with that. And he helps with the ketch and off they go, looking for lampuka, though I remember he and Oscar coming home once with an old grandfather octopus. The beast had a beak like an eagle, that old green grandad from the wrecks, grumbling and waving its arms, and we said no, take the monster back. It lay there and looked at us with disdain. A grumpy old patriarch with the sea hissing in his flesh. It will be tough as a tyre, we said, your axe couldn't cut it. And anyway, it's bad luck. This one's old enough to have met the Emperor Napoleon himself. And it has survived those Sicilian pirates in their speedboats. Think of the life it has led. When that beast dies maybe the last memory of Lord Nelson will be lost to the world. And Ahmed looked at us then with octopus eyes.

But Masso? He lives with his mother behind Our Lady of the Victories. It's a cellar like some whisky-dive but it's their home when he's not taking passengers around French Creek in his watertaxi. Masso brings that djhasja across the bay sometimes, and sometimes I go with him, or Oscar, or the African, even the moonmad Macedonian, if he promises to sit tight, and we have a good time with our rods in the summer evenings, the ocean flat and the air still warm, and flocks of songbirds crossing the bay, blackcaps and those little warblers no bigger than olive leaves, always heading away, away from us and the snarers' nets.

And maybe we play a flawt or guitar but nothing to scare the fish. It's bream we go for, slippery bream for our baskets and sometimes we're lucky, but then Masso gets worried about his mother.

What if she's fallen over? How will a bream help that? he asks.

She'll only fall over if she has another suck of that duty-free she keeps under the floorboards, Oscar will say, but all too soon it's ended and our taximan is taking the boat backwards, edging towards the walls and soon we're under the ramparts' shadow where the air is cool and purple.

Ciao, Masso, we say, and he putters and phutters back round to his mum, the lady of the victories all right, her shrine where his balls should be, the bottom of his boat full of torn up tickets.

Then there is David who lives on the ramparts above the yacht club in a room that once was a gun emplacement. Snug and dark. That's the best that can be said for it. At night he will look out at the stations of the stars all the way to Tunis. David spends his money at the tattooist in Strait Street, that little entry between the Smiling Prince tavern and the Consulate of the Grand Duchy of Luxembourg. A story is unfolding upon his back and shoulders and it concerns his greatest dream. To catch a devil fish. David has heard many stories about them, but none of us, apart from our kingly African, will ever accompany him. Why? Because he sails out for days in an old motor-boat with an oildrum of drinking water and hardly a tarpaulin to hide from the sun. David, bless him, has read the great books and his hero is Odysseus.

David, I say, beware the tales. The poets are never to be trusted. They are an eelish tribe. But that young man has decided he has a quest. We need such things, he says. A great work. A challenge and a life's undertaking. And I nod and smile and say no more. Too soon David will sleep the iron sleep.

Ciangura? His home is an attic behind the Palazzo Carafa, opposite the Societa Dante Alighieri. You must have seen it? Near the amateur football HQ. Ciangura is determined to net cerna to sell to the restaurants. His cousin is a chef and looks out for our catch. Well this Ciangura, he lives with a dumb woman, her hair is greasy as sump oil. A skinny cat, not bad looking. Or so I'm told. And jumpy as a hare. That's a poor corner now, though much of the district has become offices for notaries and advocates. You know the type. Well, this woman plays the zither and that's what you'll hear if you ever climb to Ciangura's apartment, someone's transistor in the middle flat, then this slithery zithery thing at the very top, zinging and zanging, not an atrocious sound. Not an insult to the ear, I have to say. And the sky blue in the roof.

Scibberas's idea is always to go for ceppulazza, which doesn't excite many of the others, though they sometimes agree. We always think he has an interesting life because next to him on Saint Christopher Street is a Moroccan trading company that claims to import furniture and musical instruments. But the door is covered in dust and there's few have seen it open.

Hey Skibbo, we say. What goes on?

Then he will shrug and say 'search me' and pull his boat down the steps on a set of pramwheels. But we are suspicious of that smile. It is a dolphin's smile. Because when the dolphin smiles it is thinking about something else. Well, we've heard that Scibberas and Aurelio and Ciangura sometimes help the Moroccans, lugging rugs out of vans. A bit of muscle. And as payment they are each given a pinch of hashchich.

Skibbo, we say, any fool can smell that sweet smoke. The air about you is like a dolceria. And your eyelids, Skibbo, are heavy as a goshawk's, and a dreamy look upon your face and no edge to you man, these days. No zip in your zobb.

But Skibbo will pull the boat along on its wheels and laugh and stumble and tell us of his dreams and his girl friend's dreams because they dream the same dream. And we always groan at that and shake our heads. We are experienced men. You must understand that. Men of the world. That kind of talk is bread dipped in tea. The same dream? Sop we call it here. Bloody sop.

2. The Bells

When I awake the Carmelites are chanting. Perhaps it is they who have broken my sleep. But that sound? I say to myself. That sound? I am born in bells. Their cast iron is this apartment's walls. Green, I say. A green iron sound from which there is no mercy, no mercy from these bells that roar like bulls, green bulls that roam this city at dawn and dusk and every sanctified hour between, and my bed hard as a shelf, this bed drenched in dreams and the light upon me a crust of pearls.

Yes, I say. Praise the bells. They have freed me from the madnesses of sleep. So perhaps I should walk out now and join the devout and the poor and pray for my own soul. I should stand where the bells bellow, stand in the nave of the thunderstorm and let the priests prosecute this intruder. But I tell you straight. I will never confess. Never. I've done what

I've done and I'll pay what I have to pay but I will not do God's dirty work.

3. Paradiso

I have seen her sometimes on the stair or at the Stage Door and we have exchanged greetings. Today in Leone's, there she is, a cup before her like a white bell. Her treat to herself, she says. Coffee with cardamom.

As we have the theatre in common it is easy to talk. It seems she has been a cleaner there for thirty years, starting at fifteen, like her mother before her, her mother with whom she lives in an alley under the eastern bastion.

Not much money, she smiles. But a steady job.

What's been your favourite concert? I ask.

But Manuela has never attended a concert in the theatre. Nor a play, nor any paying performance. Rehearsals? Now that's a different matter.

By the evening, I'm tired out, she says. So much dust. So many people and so much dust. There's dust in the costumes and a dune of dust in the orchestra pit. It comes from the fresco.

The painting in the cupola?

The fresco. In the paradiso, she says.

I have heard about the painting, I say.

Yes. High up amongst the blue and gold. Three hundred years old. Caravaggio, they say.

Surely not?

El Greco, then.

Never.

Oh maybe, she says. Maybe. He is looking at it now.

Who?

The Superintendent. But he's been called away.

Show me, I say.

Now?

Yes.

The theatre is always being restored. Its limestone flakes

away in a tawny scurf. Its lead leaks, its boards rot. Out in the street, Manuela takes an iron key from her bag and opens the artists' entrance. We step in darkness down a corridor and up a flight of steps. Suddenly, we are on stage.

Was there a concert last night? I ask.

Nothing.

Are you sure? I thought I heard voices. And singing.

No, nothing.

And strange music.

Manuela laughs. Manuela in her pinafore, Manuela in her slippers because her bunions hurt today. All her life Manuela's feet have suffered the island's broken steps.

The light is rosy here. The boxes above stage and along the walls are quilted in a red plush. And there is gilt everywhere, a circuitry of gold luxuriant as honeysuckle. A ladder stands in the auditorium and reaches a hundred feet into the paradiso, and yes, I am climbing, climbing a sketchy ladder towards God, out of the darkness and into the gilded light that filters in through windows like arrow slits, climbing further and Manuela laughing, Manuela whom I thought would protest, but who is laughing at me as if I was performing here for her, Manuela who has never seen a pantomime nor an oratorio, but who watches me now, Manuela who is already so far below in the black ranks of seats and I peer into the Superintendent of Singing's box and then into the Presidente's balcony and the light falls over me, a light that might devour me and no there's no going back even as I feel the ladder shudder and bend, the ladder that is really three, four, five ladders held together in aluminium brackets, a ladder that bows like bamboo, some rungs wooden and some wire and once a rung missing but I am beyond that chasm now and the dust is falling, yes, the paradiso dust that has settled upon me every time I have entered here, the dust I noted in Manuela's hair as she raised the coffee to her lips, I am ordained in that dust, as were the sopranos and the comedians, the cellists with their knees flung wide as if to receive the dust, that dust is falling past me into the abyss, and here are the nets that catch the goldleaf as it drifts out of heaven, nets of a fine silk stocking mesh with the gilt dull within that weave, dark fishscales of gold that must be counted and catalogued and replaced and the nets billow round me like webs but I shoulder through and there is paint in my mouth that tastes of lead soldiers from a lifetime ago and the ladder bends and my knees ache though all I am thinking of is the coffee in Leone's, the coffee with cardamom that Manuela urged me to try; I'm surprised you didn't know already, she had said, surprised you didn't, the cardamom and the lead soldiers within my mouth, and a knifeblade somehow upon my tongue, which might be fear, an iron tine that presses harder between my teeth even though those teeth are clenched and when I raise my eyes at last here is the ceiling and the fresco foaming so close I might touch it if I chose.

And I choose. Finger by finger I unwrap my right hand from the ladder, the ladder that is tied to two iron brackets in the ceiling and I reach up towards a hand that extends towards me, a saint's hand or even God's or maybe the skinny finger of a demon because perhaps the fresco is a depiction of hell, but angel or devil I am glad to touch this figure in the paradiso, his face an empty dial, the colour gone entirely so that only his hand remains here one hundred feet above the auditorium, and beyond that hand yet unreachable are the stars, all dark lanterns now, those stars once silver which today are mere outlines of stars. Yes, a constellation of dead stars and black planets above the gods themselves.

4. Television

Yes, I say to myself. Or rather, no. But what's certain is that it's not taken long to lose my mind. Is that something to be proud of? Perhaps I should treasure the fact.

I turn on the television. Channel One is the Government Channel. Channel Two the same. These are live broadcasts of the government's pronouncements. Channel Three is a repeat of what the government announced yesterday. Channel Four is what the government said two days ago. I zap and zap.

Then, at last. Channel Forty Two is the forecast. Here it comes.

Sea? *Confused*
Wind? *Bourgeois.*
Sun? *Indiscriminate.*
Air? *Vanishing.*
Fire? *Numb.*
Earth? *Mythic.*
Snow? *Bisexual.*
Visibility? *Salacious.*
Pressure? *Yellow.*
Tomorrow? *Xenophobic.*
Long term? *Vodka martini, no ice.*

Yes, I say to myself. Yes, yes, yes. Then, no no no no no. Then I say, or. Or or. That's it, I say. Or.

5. The Pealing

I make an appointment with the Superintendent of Bells. Because I have questions.

Why do the Carmelite church bells and the bells of the shipwreck church and the cathedral bells and St Pawlu bells and St Christopher's bells and the Lady of Damascus bells and the Victories bells not strike on the hour or the half or the quarter? And if they do strike on the hour, why do they strike the wrong hour?

The Superintendent comes to my apartment to listen. He sits there on my sofa with a saucer upon his knees. We wait. When the bells start to ring, he consults his watch. After one hour, his tea not touched, the Superintendent of Bells says he will inform the pealers' sergeant-at-arms and that officer will act. Or not, as the case might be.

There is a backlog of enquiries, he says, that must be dealt with first. Some complaints, of course. But also praise for the bells and the bellringers. Some people want more peals.

Did I know that?

There are one hundred and forty seven saints' days, he says. And that doesn't include Sundays. Also, there are victory celebrations. There are so many wars. It is lucky for you we do not celebrate the defeats. And of course the bells must be tested. Every so often bells must be brought to the boil. Bells must be allowed their bellowing, as I have heard it put. Bells must bawl. Bells are bowls. We must fill them to the brim. That is why they are bells. If bells don't ring it is surely a crime and an insult to the bellmakers' union, the bellbrokers society and campanologists everywhere. At one time, sir, we will all be summoned by bells.

You betcha, I say.

And as far as I am concerned, he says, these bells are not loud. I have visited homes where the grandparents' dentures have rattled, where the window glass has shivered, where an ikon of Our Lady was disturbed from the wall.

What about the fresco? I ask. In the theatre?

What do you mean?

It's flaking away. It's unique and priceless and it's flaking away. I blame the bells.

Surely not, says the Superintendent. Though now you mention it, the Carmelite bells are particularly...

Unbearable?

Particularly...

Deafening?

No, particularly fine bells.

Particularly loud bells, I say. With monstrous clappers. When they ring, as you've heard, it's like a hundred black-smiths hammering horseshoes.

Hmm, he says again. The fresco.

I look at the dandruff on his shoulders. The dust.

Perhaps, he says, regarding the fresco, perhaps the Department of Tintinnabulation should be informed.

6. The Soldier's Tale

There was a man I sometimes saw at Leone's on the island of lightning. We would talk, and one day he told me his story.

Yes, I escaped, he said. Came here in the bottom of a fishing boat. The crew threw me out on the north side of the island, not a crust in my pocket, not a word of the island's language in my head.

For months, maybe years I had stood in the black land. There were the stars, as thick as leopard fur. And below the stars was our platoon. You could predict each one of us: clown, psycho, clerk, coward. Which was I? Apart from such conscripts there was only one real soldier. The sergeant.

We knew that out there in the desert was the madman's army. We could see their campfires and sometimes the plastic wrappers from their rations blew into our camp. Some of our boys would lick the sugar off the cellophane. But we all understood that their army was as poor as our army, as afraid as our army, as badly-equipped as we were, our guns without bullets, our boots without laces. And we knew they were as stupid as we knew we were stupid. And like our army we knew the other army would be full of beggars and boys and pederasts.

It seemed that I was always on guard. But there was nothing to guard. We were guarding the border but the border was a straight line. On one side, a grain of sand. On the other side, another grain. I used to look at the ground where the border was written and try to understand.

Surely it should be a special place, a border? Maybe it should be a holy place. So why such straight lines? Were the emperors so bored they required their draftsmen to draw the border through mountains and mosques and grazing land, separating the kid from the goat?

No, they weren't so careless. There was oil in the north. There was oil in the south. But in the middle there was nothing. So the people from the middle stole the oil.

I patrolled the wire. Right, left, up, down. Up and down I

looked at Rigel. Rigel was the left foot of the conqueror and that was a cold light. Right, left I gazed at Betelgeuse. That star was the right shoulder of the conqueror, and I found no comfort in its urn of ash.

Out in the dark there was sometimes laughter, sometimes screaming. Just like our camp. And some nights the sergeant would appear. It had to be in darkness and he came silent as a sniper, creeping along the wire towards me.

Look, sarge, I would say. I'm on your side.

Though he did not reply his mouth would make a bubble. And then he would laugh, a dark man the sergeant, from some southern tribe, black hair on his belly and his billyclub with a bloody ferrule.

Washed was he? Where was the water to wash in the Badiet esh Sham? There was no pool there, no tarn and no tarp to trap the dew. Even in that dry air he smelt like a mule.

Whose side? he would whisper.

And I would look at the whipcord in his cock and see that the border ran even there.

Whose side? he would hiss.

Your side, sarge, I would answer, the wind blowing, the sugar papers trapped on the wire, Orion and the madman's stars almost overhead.

7. Swiftsure

There is a man lives in Eagle Street who deserted from the Royal Navy many years ago. I sometimes see him in an upstairs window where he will sit in the mornings, a thin man with a sallow face, a birdcage that holds a linnet beside him.

Manuela tells me stories about this Mr Swiftsure, as we sit over our coffee and cardamom during her breaks. Last night in my room, sleep had been particularly heavy. I had awoken with difficulty, a cabaret of weeping in my head. Yesterday there had been children's voices in the theatre. A school party I supposed, although I knew the place was closed. And whispering too. A campaign of whispering, transparent voices floating to earth like cranefly wings.

Swiftsure has worked in the victualling yard and made himself useful during the sieges, even after losing a foot to a musketball. Once he ferried laudanum and lemon juice to the lazzaretto so people are inclined to turn a blind eye, even with a bounty on the old smuggler's head.

Not me, whispers Manuela. I hate old Swiftsure.

Why?

He has hides all over the island. And a little popgun. Swiftsure shoots birds. He will sit in his hide all day for the chance of a potshot. Eagles, pigeons, the tiny birds that pass in spring, he shoots them all.

She leans closer.

He's a snarer too. A poacher. Like the rest of them he uses snares to catch birds alive. But I think of him in his hides. Oh, so beautifully camouflaged. You'll pass a yard away and not notice there is green canvas in the branches and a little man sitting in the scorpion grass with his gun cocked. You know…

What?

He could be with us in this room. And you'd not notice him. Of all the snarers, Swiftsure's the craftiest. He can be invisible.

Now coincidentally, but the island of lightning is full of coincidences, I encounter Swiftsure this afternoon. He is in the street, whimpering after the linnet that has fallen from its cage. I find the bird in a drain and capture it, wings bedraggled, its eye a raspberry seed.

Ta boss, says Swiftsure. Ta very much. The old King o' Naples wouldn't last long with these cats. You must come up, boss. Come up for a drink.

Swiftsure pours cactus juice from a stone jug with a mitred lip.

To his lordship.

Pardon?

Nelson of course. What other lord is there in these parts?

I look around. There are stuffed birds everywhere. A bee

eater sits inside the door, a plover in black and gold stencilling hovers from a wire overhead. On the table, otherwise covered with papers, wineglasses and an evil-looking nimcha, stands a brass astrolabe. Swiftsure follows my gaze.

Arab work, he says. Very useful if you want to say a few Hail Marys toward Mecca.

Do you use it?

Oh yes. It's a stardome too. I go out mostly at night. Get away from the lights see. Just bob about out there and look at the globe then study the stars themselves. Sometimes I can even tell where I am. Watch this.

Swiftsure closes the curtain and strikes a light, applying it to the well of oil within the globe. In the gloom it starts to glow and the star holes cut in the copper make a smoky constellation. From its cage on the balcony the linnet starts to sing.

You're honoured, Swiftsure says. Old King o' Naples doesn't do much of that these days. He's a good old bird.

We stand together in the dusk listening to its song. Then he touches the globe.

See this star. Its name is Antares. The pride of Scorpio. And if you look at it as I do, through a spyglass, it's exactly the same colour as this. A ruby in the night. That's Antares. With a sapphire close beside it too, because Antares has a pale companion. You'll have to come out one night and see for yourself

I'd like that.

Learn to set the equipment, laughs Swiftsure. You know, his lordship used to look for Antares most nights when in these waters. Can't see it a lot of the time in England.

The poacher pours another round.

Good health, I propose.

Well, maybe. I always say this stuff's the only thing that keeps me going.

The linnet like a clockwork bird, has stopped its song. Swiftsure and I stand together in the dark, the furnace of stars between us.

You know, he says, after Trafalgar they sent his lordship home stood up in a barrel of grog. Pickled the poor sod, they did. Buried the bugger in brandy. And no kidding, sometimes I know just how old Horatio must have felt. Cheers, boss.

8. The First Couple

One day Omar and I are leaving the Piccadilly when a man hails us from a balcony. We climb his stairs and part a bead curtain.

Salutations, says Omar. How the devil are you? Now, may I perform the introductions?

There are two men before us in the tiny room. Behind them the balcony is set with two plastic chairs and a table.

This is Mercurius, says Omar. A man extends his hand, a greyhaired man with a stubbly beard, the apron over his jeans covered in paint. His clothes too are discoloured, also the fingers I take.

The room is full of canvases, always, it seems, of the sea, the sea at dawn with the mist upon it, the midnight sea where the island's lights are reprinted in yellow, a sea teeming with whales and dolphins and creatures that can never have existed. And ships too, the ships that have visited the island since men ventured into the deeps.

And this is Gloriana.

Pleasured to you, says the second man, hair in toffee paper twists, his kimono pumiced with cigarette burns.

We share their supper of bread and blood oranges, Gloriana tipping fino into himself, the rest of us coffee.

You knows what Omar calls us? he cackles. Dido and Anaeas. How grand he makes us sound. And how old.

Surely Gloriana is grand enough, I say.

He shrugs and blows smoke. Ah yes, darlings. The virgin queen. She has been a role model once but I seem to have departed from the script.

We had an unfortunate incident, says Mercurius.

Unfortunate? shrieks his partner. These sailor boys come up the stairs as good sailor boys does, but I knows they is trouble in storage.

Inebriated, says Mercurius.

Steaming, darlings. Pisticated. Anyways, to cuts the short stories shorter, they kicks the place to kingdom come.

Paintings over, easel broken, the lot, said Mercurius.

Pushes Dido here over too. Fat lots of good Dido heres is. Not Caravaggio, are you, darling? Where's Caravaggio when I need him? Not seen at his lodgings a long times now.

Yes, they roughed Old Glory up something chronic, said Mercurius. Dangled the little darling over the balcony. Didn't they, you silly ox?

That's how I gets the shiner, says Gloriana. Losing thirty-five cents, too. Hanging there, I sees the wolves in the street, their greedy eyes below me in the dark.

Problem is, says Mercurius looking at me, our street used to be well known.

Notorious, smiles Omar.

But times, they changes, says Gloriana. Supplies, demands.

Unfair competition, says Mercuius.

So our friends here are the last, says Omar to me. Of the line. To perform, shall we say, a public duty.

Too true, says Gloriana, looking round. We soothes. We consoles. We gets the steam out of the radiator and boys I tells you that steam has got to gets out of it somehow. But blimeys yes, as you well knows, there's no problems with sailors. Sailors with problems, yes honey. But not the other ways about. I counts ships sometimes under my sleep. The Simon, the Santa Theresa…

The Matrona…

The Punta la Gaviota

Good ship the Punta, says Mercuius.

The Viver Atun Uno…

The Baltic Breaker.

Oo yes, says Gloriana. All those happy Finlandings. I had one in here, you knows, and he wouldn't stop crying. Hanini, I says. Here's grapes. Here's pommies. But you knows what he wants? He wants cold. He wants dark. He wants to sleep it all days and gets up it all nights. He wants it all backs to fronts. Look, I says, here's a pin for the pommie. Stick it theres. And theres. But it's no uses, so he goes back early. Or late. I don't even cares no more.

Anyway, says Mercuius. We have news. Which is the reason for bringing you up. Look.

And both he and Gloriana show off the rings they have bought one another, wiggling their fingers with the two gold bands.

The Bishop of the Blue Lagoon came last week, he continues. But an official visit, you understand.

Ceremony very good, sighs Gloriana. I cries right through it. And, you knows? We are the firsts, I think. We are the firsts to be ever on the islands and so will be even since.

9. Tiny Gods

It's a small island and I have become used to meeting the same people and exchanging greetings. But there is one man whom I see taking coffee on the ramparts and surveying the ocean who is differently familiar. One morning I decide to act. I take my cup to the next table on the bastion and look out. The Lambusa of Limasol is entering harbour and an old ketch is leaving on an expedition for trigger fish.

Bonju, I say. A wonderful morning.

The man turns to me.

How are you these days? he smiles.

I look closely at him then.

The last time we saw each other, he says, I believe I was crying. You might think that a difficult thing to admit. But it no longer matters.

We're alive, Mohammed.

He lifts his cup in a brief toast.

Remember that hotel room in the madman's capital? I ask.

Yes, he replies. You and your companion laid out the money on the bed. Black dinars I wouldn't wipe my arse with. Royal Jordanian pounds that were more like it. But no dollars, my friend. Not a George Washington to be seen. And I needed dollars. All that work I had done. All the special services.

But the government paid you, I say.

Pistachio shells. But to repeat, it doesn't matter now.

How did you get away?

From the insanity? Surprisingly easily.

We order more coffee. The ketch has disappeared, the Cypriot cargo boat is tying up below us at two of the castiron capstans askew on the quay.

Do you know? says Mohammed. I was in a restaurant in Amman when that fool, the Information Minister, came on television and said there were no Americans. And no American tanks.

What's that then? the journalists asked. There was a Challenger coming down El Rashid Street behind this oaf. A Challenger tank with a barrel long as a palm tree.

Oh, pardon me, gentlemen, says the Minister, I have an urgent appointment. And he disappears.

How we all laughed in that café. Or maybe I was still crying, but the coffee was very strong. Yes, that café was an excellent place. There were CIA there, braying and bragging, but I wasn't afraid. Small fry, you see, I was never more than that. My picture wasn't on their screens. Not one of the playing cards, not even close. A different game entirely.

How did you get here?

Mohammed smiles again and points into the dock. There are people disembarking from the Lambusa, filthy sailors, an old man, a woman with a suitcase.

Well, maybe Amman was a little fraught. So I hired a pick-up and took my bags to Beirut where I have a friend. Then, when the money started to come in, I decided to travel. See the world. I have a pleasant apartment here, you will have to come over.

So money's no problem? It used to be.

Mohammed looks hard at me. He is a man of about sixty in a linen suit, a shirt with a frayed collar.

I apologise, he says. For crying, that is. How unedifying it must have seemed.

Those were strange times.

No, my friend. Those were good times. Well, better times, despite the embargo. These are the strange times. The dangerous times. He whose name we could never speak, he whose photograph was in every room, he was maybe not so mad after all.

You miss those times?

The certainties? Yes. Being able to sit in a restaurant or walk down the street without some imbecile blowing his useless carcass up beside you? Yes I miss those times.

How do you live?

He looks at me tolerantly.

Remember the museum? I had it opened especially for you and your friend.

It was unbelievable, I say.

Before I left I paid it a visit. And then another visit.

It was marvellous, I say.

Mohammed produces his wallet and from it a plastic wrapper three inches square. From this he takes a piece of bubblewrap. Within it might be a dark coin.

It's a stamp, he says. Or a seal. A stamp, a seal.

I look at the broken disc which he doesn't let me touch. There are designs of antelopes upon it and men who might be hunters.

Pretty isn't it, he smiles. And, guess what?
What?

It is six thousand years old.

He sits back, the bubblewrap on the table between us, the

disc catching the sun. It waits like a tip for the waiter.

Such a pretty thing. And there is so much more, so much you wouldn't believe it. You see, we Mesopotamians are a civilised people. Six thousand years ago we had artists and craftsmen and kings who craved such fine art. When your people were rubbing sticks together.

You looted the museum?

Of course not. I went with a friend who knows Nineveh, who understands how Babylon and Ur were built. Who knew what wouldn't be missed and what the country could afford to lose. Oh, we were careful in that. We were scrupulous.

We both look out. A dredger called the Sapphire is coming in with its gravel and mud.

See, says Mohammed, we walked down the aisles of the museum and we were the only people there. Just like when you paid your visit. No wardens. No guardians, no professors muttering or students sketching. And no glass on the floor as there soon would be.

We came to a hall. In a cabinet was a copper mask, a bearded king's head, and the king's beard was cut in curls and ringlets in the copper, and the king's eyes were hollow and there was a copper crown upon his head. But his lips were a woman's lips, red and royal and alive. I looked at that king in the twilight and thought, yes, I could love that man. For that man is an imperial leader, maybe a cruel man, maybe a murderer of his people, a sacrificer of children, a lunatic, a psychopath. But here he is, here is the king. After five thousand years, here is the king.

And my hands were on that cabinet and I said we must take this, we must. And you know what my friend did? He touched me on the shoulder. Such a beautiful touch. It explained everything. And the passion passed. And we walked on through the museum and we left Nebuchadnezzar's dragons and the Assyrian magicians with their square whiskers and we took what would not be missed. Tiny gods. It was only the tiny gods we took. The smallest gods who never really mattered. Not gold but alabaster gods. As tiny as chessmen, those gods. My gods now. And seals like this. Some tiles from Babylon. And a red cheetah that fits my hand.

Because I am silent, Mohammed thinks I am critical.

I saved them, he says. I saved them for the world. Where is the great king now? Where are the lions of Uruk or the golden bulls? Where are the chariots? Where are the tablets with the world's first writing? Gone my friend, gone with the smugglers who lacked my scruples. Gone with the idiots who exchanged eternity for cigarettes. I sell what I took to dealers who make one hundred times, one thousand times the money I could ever do. But my tiny gods will be safe in Damascus or Los Angeles when the rest of it is dust in the street.

Yes, I say. I agree with you. And I wish I had done the same.

Another time, he says.

You mean for coffee?

No, says Mohammed. It was all another time.

10. The Prophet's Garden

Quickly I've learned that this island is a bad place to fall asleep. Because it is difficult to wake. Sometimes I will sit up in bed at noon or later, bewildered by the dreams that began on the first night and still continue. But often the dreams are forgotten immediately, becoming I suppose a kind of dark dream humus in which other dreams will flourish.

One afternoon I wake still delirious. The music is playing again. It was part of my slumber but I can still hear it, the silverish music made by wires and gourds, hear it even after I rub my eyes, take a glass of sweet tea.

And the dream is clear. I am in a garden surrounded by minarets. Beyond us lies a rocky region where the wind pilfers the grass. A clockwork bird is singing, a muezzin playing prayers at a mixing desk. I see a man who bears milk to a minaret, a man carrying two pails of milk climbing the ziggurat steps. It is dusk and I am on my hands and knees searching for coriander. As it is too dark to see the herb's constellations, those tiny flowers on their long stems, I have to rub the leaves of all the plants that grow there.

I know that if I touch its leaves the coriander's perfume will eke into the night. In the dream the mosque's shadow lies over the plot like a fortress fallen on this pauper's ground. It seems the land has been given to the poor that they might grow food and not starve. So maybe that is why I feel safe there. Because I am not threatened in the dream. Confused, yes, but not terrified.

Because there I am, smelling the dew, a dew-drinking animal with my face in the grass, a dog, a dungbeetle, safe in the prophet's garden, sunflower seeds stuck to my soles.

11. The Storm

At last, after an hour's search, I find where the rain is entering. But the ceiling of my room is high and it's impossible to mend the hole. So the rain will enter where it will and fill the saucepans I have placed on the floor, fill the jars, the plastic bucket. And such rain. Explosive drops that detonate on the lofts that surround my apartment, that echo on the theatre's dome, that run along the walls.

For a few moments I brave one of the theatre's flat roofs, climbing out naked through a trap door into the night. Lightning on the sea is salt on a fire. It turns green and burns blue.

Yet most of the lightning is silver as magnesium ribbon. It passes in a river over the sky forming deltas on the horizon towards Tripoli, exploding in snowstorms, dying, coming back. And such thunder. The thunder is greater than the bells. But the bells too are ringing, the Carmelite bells only yards away across the street. I can see them in the lightning, honouring some approximation of the hour and its quarters.

But when the thunder claps the bells are beaten. And now the storm is overhead so that thunder and lightning arrive together and the rain falls straight as piano wire, finding nailcracks and unleaded joints between the rafters to pour into my apartment, falling on my bed and my papers and my glossy poster for *Cosi fan Tutte*, soaking my bread and watering my wine.

But there's something else. A different sound. Even here on the roof with the aerials and washing lines, I can hear music. When I woke I was sure it was the thunder that had disturbed me. Or the bells.

Yet perhaps it was this strange and windswept music that comes to me now, a human voice praying, pleading, some unnameable instrument that has captured the sound of rain falling into rain.

Downstairs, I consult the theatre programme. Just as I thought. Nothing scheduled last night or this morning. No concert or rehearsal in these small hours. The theatre should be dark as my room. But the music, like the rain, enters where it will, praying, pleading, a storm of sorts, a fever maybe, a silveriness alive inside my head.

12. The Thrush

Here's a spell I've learned. Mix sour wine and stale bread. Then feel the world warm. But I don't cut the bread. I tear it. The flesh comes away in my hand like grass with its roots and crumbs of earth. Or limestone dust from the walls of this theatre where I live, my room high on its north side, and my life more theatrical by the minute. But with Samuel Beckett doing the writing.

Now what's that? Somebody knocking.

How dishevelled I look, I think as I open up. Unshaven, uncombed, bare chested too because the day is humid and the fans make little difference. There might be bread in my teeth. I must look like a dog disturbed at a stolen meal.

A man stands in the doorway. I know what he is going to say.

My costume? he demands. For *Cosi*?

Cosi fan Tutte costumes on the next floor down, I reply. Come with me.

And I take him along the corridor and put on the light because even in daylight this is a dingy place. Doing this is easier than explaining where the costumier's is, and I lead him down to the door marked Stage Door, and I rap for him and he thanks me and I return.

What a world awaits that chorister: collections of Ruritanian extravagance, rags of old pantomimes, armour, haloes, Saturn and its rings on invisible wire, a lifesize black and white cow, a breed never seen on this island.

All week I have followed the rehearsals. The great themes have swept up through this labyrinth and stopped and started again and been halted in a grinding of cello strings as the maestro sobs at the fools in the pit.

Was it ever different? I say to myself. Did Mozart tear his hair or did the music run seamlessly through him like candle-light on the Danube? And no, I will not come to the performance. All week I have heard the production taking shape, the chorus carrying into the small hours, the baton cracking like a pistol shot. Everything that happens in the theatre happens here.

So I get on with my dog's breakfast. The bread and the wine. The loaf as sweet as a lemon leaf. But the wine? Sometimes I drink from the bottleneck. Or I pour the wine into a bowl and soak the bread if its crust is hard. Because I've found these loaves sometimes turned to rock, the rye especially a splinter of basalt. But the wine wins. It always will. Now the bread lies in its black petals. Dreamfood I call it. All that's left of last week's loaf.

The baker is a man-child who has lived in the bakery all his life. His mother is the crone at the hatch. When she offers my few cents change I always wave it away and she whistles in admiration, whistles like one of the thrushes that dive from the ramparts. And I smile at her but realise that sarcasm from the old is harder to swallow than ancient bread.

That's why I prefer the wine shop in Zachary Street. I take a bottle there and the girl does not dip the jug as I thought she might but fills it with a ladle. The wine is cheap. At first I thought the price a mistake, but no, she assured me, no, put that coin away, and that one too. Look. I need only this one and this one. And okay, this one with the thrush upon it, our blue rock thrush, *il merill*, a bird seldom seen now because of the snarers' nets.

And such wine it is. Black as the girl's eyes watching me as I watch her dipping and pouring and dipping. Yes, the same darkness in the barrel as in her gaze. Because this wine is inscrutable even in candlelight, this wine my tarry physic, warm in the room as the girl's hand might be. I touched it once. I touched her hand and she did not withdraw. But the jug was full and I was scrabbling for coins, for the coin with the thrush upon it. Yes, a rare bird now as everybody says.

13. Counting the Fireflies

If Omar is not telling tourists about the island's past, standing on the steps of a palazzo or in a cobbled yard where blue bees crawl through hibiscus, I ask for an hour, or an afternoon, of his time. Often, he agrees, and I feel honoured.

Yet so far he has said nothing about the gods. Yes, he tells me of the baroque churches. Of the Renaissance art. But that's not what interests me. I'm not that kind of scholar.

Today he takes me to a place I must have passed a score of times, yet never noticed. Under the western ramparts the walls are a maze of tunnels used by fishermen and lovers and the klandestini. Down a flight of steps we stop in shadow. There is a string of washing hung against an entrance, and above this door are two eyes painted blue and white, and the word *Caccarun* in flaking paint.

Omar leads the way, parts the shirts and vests on the line and beckons me inside. It is a small room, perhaps a kitchen. There are a table and two chairs and shelves of jars and bottles. The room is dark, so dark I cannot see that around the wall this space continues. Omar leads on. The room becomes a tunnel. Ahead a candle is burning. There are two diesel drums with a piece of driftwood between them. In the gloom, I think, someone might be sitting at this board.

Wine? asks Omar, and he himself lifts a bottle and two dusty glasses from a shelf.

Where are we? I ask.

Under the bastion, says my guide. It's time you met the Phoenician. Hey Nannu, your health.

Omar is toasting the shadow in the corner. I look closer. There is a man there with hair the colour of a spiderweb. An empty glass waits before him. Omar offers to pour him wine, Omar already the host, Omar the leader. But the figure places a palm over his cup. This man is very frail. In the candlelight his skin is yellow.

No hurry at all, smiles Omar. Nannu has waited a long time. He will wait longer. But you, sir, you should learn more.

Of course, I say. I'm here to learn. But...

Then listen, says Omar. We're in the warren here. These tunnels run a long way. Above us is a palace of many rooms and in its history it has been many things. Now, it's a kind of hotel. Sixteen women live there, not as many as before. But if you would know the island, you must know them.

It's less the present, I say. Than the past. The ancient days. And the...

But Omar holds up his hand.

First, the lovely Rusatia. Ask her, and she will dress as a priest for you. Or the Emperor himself. As a gladiator if such is your taste. No, she is never without callers.

Callidrome is a little older. She keeps a goat in her suite and feeds it radishes. It is tied to her bed with a toga chord and Callidrome rouges its white cheeks and puts lipstick on its nannygoat lips. Yes, Callidrome's goat is a beautiful creature, its eyes like dates. Once she gave it cocaine and she swore it spoke monk's Latin.

Fortunata is inseparable from her mother. They are, I

suppose, a team. Once mummy put a love potion in the communion wine, then they waited in their room. The first to knock was the Bishop of the Blue Lagoon, and soon a school-teacher with his class dinner money. Yes, powerful medicine.

Now Fabia, she has style. She drinks ouzo from Milos and listens to Cole Porter songs. Ah, she whispers, I was his muse. In love with the night mysterious? Of course. He came here you know. To this island. Ah Mr Porter, sang Fabia. What shall I do? Night and day, you are the one. That's Fabia's best line, I think. Of course, it didn't last. Poor Porter with his limp and his money? The hotel was no place for him and Fabia such a demanding child. But for a while they got along. They were artists, you see. He could no more stop writing his music than Fabia turn down one million Turkish lire for a tick of her eyebrow pencil. People like that can never switch off. Because you should never retire. Ask old Nannu here. Still keeping a bar. So Fabia stays working. What should she be doing? Watching the island's TV? As she will say, I am a witness, as are all artists.

Nica is always in demand because she owns the strongest mosquito spray. *Pif Pif,* I think it is called. Yes, a powerful poison that gives those swampflies no chance. But as to losing blood, doesn't little Nica have that all her own way? How sweet, Nica will say, after her pearly whites have done their job. Advocates taste of palm oil, she tells the other girls. And MPs of mothballs. Her favourites of course are the orchestra from the theatre. Apparently, violinists are salty as the Ligurian deeps. Oh, what blood, little Nica will say. I can taste the music in it.

Felicia drinks like no other. Her tipple is anis, which has deranged many a fine mind. Men often challenge her to a bulb of wine. Always Felicia wins. How? Because she doesn't swallow. The wine simply disappears into her gullet, though sometimes of course, I can hear it sloshing about when I place my ear to her belly, a belly dark as a communion plate. Yes, little Felicia, outdrinking the lascars, the Ark Royal stokers tattooed like Scythians, the trireme oarsmen still in their chains. How often have I seen her hands in their pockets or lifting a greasy tarboosh while they slept it off? Often, brother. Oh yes.

Cressa and Drauca work together for safety's sake. They come from Siricusa and know all the wiles of the dockside trash who want to try their luck. But one day, they were duped. Some old fool offered an IOU. He swore the next day, or the next, he'd have the brass. Together they tipped him upside down and found only grapeseeds in his suit. So they christened him with the chamber pot. No credit notes, no plastic, no Albanian squindarkas are their rules of business. Couldn't he read?

Mula is from the island. Her father makes brandy from prickly pears, and delivers a cask of it to the hotel every month. So the girls look after Mula, who cannot read, but is kind and plump and sunburned. A friendly girl. And the brandy? Rotgut. But cut it with luminata and they can stay sober at least an hour.

Now Helpis's specialty is hashchich. On her door and her website is the sign of the snake that swallows its own tail. Her shift is the blue of michaelmas daisies, and Helpsis is suitably melancholy.

As to Ianuaria, she speaks some dialect that no-one understands. Maybe she comes from Durrazo or Izmir, tough cities. Yes, the girls are a United Nations all by themselves. But those opaque vowels are no matter when she begins her love talk. Then she is the oriole the snarers crave. Yes, with her words, Ianuaria can make anyone disgorge their soul. Her tongue is a goldsmith's anvil all right. Where did that woman learn to speak such a language? Such whispering behind her boudoir door.

Faustilla? Dear Fausty's tongue is pierced with a ball bearing. It serves as a clapper for the bells that God cannot ring. So who better to serenade the priest, who has brought wine with honey and whose birretta is crushed under his fat arse?

And I know Palindrome as well as any. She is white as gesso and looks like a ghost. In her cupboard once I found the following: a charioteer's whip; sea holly; a barbed wire torque; a packet of angel dust; Vallium; blindfolds; scarabs; a map of the port of Alexandria; a stone jug of raki, pale green as I recall, and a letter from the Caliph. Oh yes, she is known in high places is our Palindrome.

Restituta wears a veil. A gorgeous hoodwinker she. Who do you favour, sir? she will ask her regulars. Am I your Dominican today? Or your grateful poor Clare? Such admirable humility. You see, Restituta has truly been a nun. But it was a roofless convent with cactus in the garden. The well had collapsed. She came here, to the island of lightning, from Kriti, where she had already learned much of her science.

And Felicia? A Nubian princess they say. Experiencing interesting times. She keeps a panther, and this beast has a shrivelled leg. As a deterrent to intruders it lives on the roof, shitting in an old roasting tin filled with torn up *Gazzetta della Sport*.

Yes, smiles Omar. They live above us. It's one of my jobs to help them out with the money. And to learn their stories of course, because all the girls are great raconteurs. What can I do with these? Nica might ask. That Moroccan in the Hugo Boss suit paid in dirhams. So I take them, as I take the dinars and the kroons and the lecs and the forints and the tolars and the dollars Canadian and turn them into money the girls can understand. A lovely family, I hope you agree. My fireflies I call them. How they glow.

14. The Wedding Dress

Today I come to a district I have not visited before. The streets are narrow here, the balconies almost touching. And there's no-one about, no-one in all this crowded city, nothing but the usual famished cats, and a linnet in a cage on a balcony, rouge-headed little harlot singing in the abandoned afternoon.

I stop on a flight of steps. The wall above is covered in bleached paintwork, devotional works that picture local saints, pale men and women exhausted by time or their passion, the blues and yellows almost drained from their robes. At a balcony above the saints hangs a bushel of dead grasses and the leaves of a salt tree that has dried to a negative of itself.

Above this balcony is strung a line of washing like a tattered gonfalon. I look at the garments pegged there, all the colour of the city's stone, stonedust in the creases of the shirts and stonedust in the shift hems, stonedust in the folds of the jerseys and the jalibayahs, stonedust covering the veils.

I look more closely. A wedding dress is hanging there, a grey gown exploding like one of last summer's cornsheaves, stonedust in its folds and flounces and its bodice embroidered with stony sequins. Behind these clothes the windows of the apartment are shut but something has been written on the glass.

I peer through the leprous underwear at the letters and spell them out and spell again, useless as they are to me as the linnet's heartbroken song.

15. The King

I see the old man has wandered from his house again. Or from whatever hole in the ramparts he inhabits. In hospital pyjamas he stands on the cobbles, scratching his chest, his cock, that inflamed member red as a radish. Under his breath the old man murmurs a love song, a lullaby. Or is it some warning?

I step closer. Yes, he is muttering about dogs, how the brave and the beautiful will be eaten by dogs, unspeakable battlefield curs that lick heroes' blood and gnaw the bellies and balls of dead warriors whose golden greaves have been stolen by the thieves and whores, thick as horseflies, that follow all armies, smelling death and the must of riven exchequers, the air heavy with such perfume.

There is badger-bristle on his cheeks, his chest collapsed and hairless. This man reminds me of someone I might see where I used to live. This other man would hurry through my town, his shirt unbuttoned and cap crooked, his eyes rolling, this other man racing every morning on an impossible errand, the news he brought too terrible to communicate.

But this man does not race. Here he stands, mumbling about dogs. Perhaps someone will come and take him away but maybe he has run out of someones, as must we all. Yes, here he stands with the sea before him and the Maria Dolores coming into harbour and the Anchor Bay and the Martzaiola departing our shore and the pigeons clinging to the fortress brick. For this is honey-coloured Troy. And here stands Priam, shaking his pizzle at the Greeks.

16. Sigmundo

There is a saint carved from the mast of a scuppered scutch. Peter in effigy is whiskered with grime, the gilt on him dusty as mothwings. But Peter is celebrated here.

There's no plaque to give his proper name so I will call him Sigmundo. Yet who is or was Sigmundo? All I find, and all I see, are the skull and a casket of relics, bones above a tomb in the shipwreck church.

Ah, Sigmundo, I whisper. How goes it, brother?

Or, Good morning, Sigmundo. Do you hear the rain outside, a torrent down the steps of this city and bouncing off the lead on the cupolas above us? Please, tell me what you know, Sigmundo, and what you see with those hollow eyes, bony cupolas themselves those sockets.

But was it not the monks' trick to roast a pig and gnaw the bones white and then proclaim them the holy scaffolding of a saint? Surely I'm not talking to a boar, Sigmundo? Or a red titted sow famished for her farrow?

Or maybe you are a rabbit, Sig? So many rabbits are

served on this island, roasted, stewed a week in garlic and crusty wine. The peasant cuisine. But what peasant could wait a week. Please prove to me Sigmundo that you are not a bucket of bones and that I retain traces of sanity.

But, sir, I honour you. The Luftwaffe didn't get you, nor the skull-embroidered legions. And you are so beautiful in this sacred twilight, a goblet dressed in madriperla. And, best of all, there's no-one near the saint's inglenook to hear me talking to a bone.

Well, such are my rituals in this city, where I live quietly and attend to my duties. A coffee at Leone's and a word with Sigmundo in his crystal. And truly, yes, I would like to take him outside to the rampart to watch the sea breaking below. Because the light would have you gasping, Sig. Maybe I'd offer you Raybans.

Yes my friend, there in your aquarium, staring over the Libyan Sea that spits like an iron's hotplate, tell me which way did the galleys come?

Ah yes, the same way the ferries do now. Because, as you know, this is where all trajectories meet. East and west merge upon our Phoenician rock, and a hollow rock it is, hollow with caves, and churches in caves and casbahs in caves and taverns in caverns and calabashes in caves and jewellers' and haber-dasheries and harlotries in caves. Yes an island of caves, Sigmundo. Maybe you hear the tide beneath our feet?

So let's wait here a while and realise we have come to the centre of things. A rock on the horizon. That's us, my friend. A limestone mote in Africa's eye. But think of our forebears. Odysseus was here once, and Bloodaxe too, while Philip's fleets brought figs and falcons. So gaze with me here, Sigmundo. And realise the world is looking at us.

17. Waiting for the Barbarians

A cup of the warm south, says my friend. But nicely chilled.

We take our seats and here she comes, a pale girl, a goose of a girl, a gorgeous gooney girl with a mouth like a goldfish, a tall and serious girl with slender neck and hair in a tortoise-shell clasp plaited down her back.

Now she ghosts towards us and now she ghosts away, this servant who will bring our glasses. My friend is astonished. The girl cannot speak the island's language. Where can she have come from? She a servant, too. A minion.

It's written right through her, he says. From one of the so called republics to the north. One of those insane ragbags of counties and impoverished commotes. That's where she's from.

Since the island entered the confederation such outlandish types are seen more frequently. But the bar owner is a cruel man. He shouts at the goosey girl. He makes her stand in a corner and clean the necks of the ketchup bottles. Maybe he will make her do other things.

Wild dogs in the squares. The Presidents all turnip farmers. Black magic in the back streets and the children not in school but the uranium mines. And the old men drinking eau-de-cologne and antifreeze. It's true. They worship salamanders there. And now, here they come, here come the salamander-worshipping eau-de-cologne drinkers. And they're unstoppable.

I look at the girl. She dribbles rice grains into salt cellars. At an empty table she reads the Borges olive oil bottle label and the Borges vinegar bottle label. And very slowly, as if she has recognised an old friend, she begins to smile.

18. Klandestins

One day I arrange to meet Omar at Nannu's place. When I arrive no-one but Nannu is present. I wait in a darkness lit by one red candle on the board. Outside, the light is shattering and the sea wild, a curdled milk. Inside, it is midnight.

As usual the Caccarun is silent and I pour my own drink. I wonder whether it is his laundry that hangs over the entrance. The Caccarun must have better things to think about than personal hygiene, and I too must look unkempt, a week's bristles, and sour wine in my armpits, appropriate for the tavern of the two eyes. If I need a pexpex, there's a slop pot. But no lavaman that I've seen. My research is not going well.

At last Omar arrives.

Has the catastropher been talking to you? he asks.

Nannu?

Wars and invasions, Nannu knows when. And why. Ask him, man. He'll tell you when the rains are due. The new rains. He understands how hot it will become. Nannu has predicted how far the tide will creep up the ramparts. And yes, Nannu has even counted how many people are moving towards us, across the desert, over the waves. Towards us now, at this moment. He can see them all. Or rather…

Omar takes a shell from a shelf and gives it to the old man.

What do you hear, Nannu?

The old man remains silent.

Does he hear the sea? I ask.

I'll tell you what Nannu hears, says Omar. Ships' bells. So much louder than church bells. And so many more of them. Many men with many oars. That's what Nannu hears in the shell. The sound of oars. The galleys coming this way, the galleons with bells in their rigging, the gondolas, the gharbiels, the lazzarettos, the cruise liners. And the king astride his driftwood shaking that five pointed fork.

But does he hear the gods? I whisper

Maybe Omar doesn't hear.

Occasionally on my travels I pass a derelict barrakka on the west side. The blocks in the wall have shrunk and the building is unsafe. So there are plenty of places to stow away, to squat, to put a bedroll in the dust.

I suppose that's where I see most of the illegals, in the holes in the walls, holes such as the fishermen use. The ramparts are a honeycomb, entrances and dead ends and who knows how deep a labyrinth it all is. And there they are, rats in the rock, or in and out like flying foxes, because I've seen the bats too in the dusk on their own journeys, sharing their chambers now with these unfortunates.

Many's the time I've seen klandestins go in one hole and come out another. I've looked in too and seen dried palm leaves covering blankets, old clothes, yoghurt pots with rainwater, stale bread from the wheelies, bags of olives.

Because that's what these people do. Pick up olives. They sit under the olive trees and fill a bag, green going black, medicinal-tasting olives, most of the crop already soft and trodden to oil under the benches.

Who's going to buy? I always wonder. There are more olives than cockroaches on the island. More olives than children and there are children everywhere, hanging from tenement windows, bobbing still in the sea before me, the coal-coloured sea with clouds massing in the north. The coral is black now and the fishes invisible.

So slight in the sun are those slim fishes that silver the eye as light stuns time. Yes the fishes have vanished. But who will buy olives when they can pick the olives themselves? There are olives everywhere.

Yet that is what the klandestins do. They pick olives and look at olives as if they have never seen olives before. Maybe they haven't. Perhaps olives are a strange fruit to these people.

Takes all sorts, I suppose. Perhaps they don't know the olives need to be soaked in brine. Soaked for weeks and even then they're not ready. They'll have to learn the hard way.

Who are they, these visitors? I ask Omar. A troupe of outcasts from the desert?

Everyone comes to the island of lightning, he says. Eventually. The Greeks in their gold breeks, Palestinian farmers whose peach trees are full of cluster bombs. They all find themselves adrift, and the currents bring them here.

We go to the highest rampart and look out. The sky is dark

and there are lanterns lit.

The rafts will come ashore in the night, says Omar. They don't have long to wait. You can imagine the passengers. Pregnant women who had never seen the sea before their journey, teachers, students, the brave, the mad.

Think of them now out on the ocean, their skins indigo in this light. Behind one another one, and behind him yet more. What if a wave takes a child from the stern? Who would know? When the snake steals the chick does the mother remember? Swallowed whole, it was never there.

Why do the superintendents let them in? I ask.

The island's grown old, he says. It's full of old men. And women. Old men are like cicadas, telling all they know. Children are the same. We are talkers now, not doers. Not warriors. We're cicadas on a tree. And ugly as cicadas. No-one listens so we sing louder. Who can tell when one of us falls because the racket is the same. And if we could learn from cicadas we would have already done so.

You wish to contact the ancients? You wish for the gods? Oh yes, I know what you wish. Those voices in our heads? Maybe those are the gods' voices. Certainly they are the cicadas. Dream sounds. The dreams of old people with the sheets up to their chins and their teeth chattering. We should honour the cicadas.

But the gods, I say.

The gods? Yes, it is always the gods with you.

Then he smiles.

Here, says Omar. For you.

He gives me a poster, old paper, cracked and stained.

There are names on it, a concert advertised for the theatre. But there's no time, no date. Abdallah Ali will play the santur; Sha'ubi Ibraham and Hassan Ali the djoze; Abdul Razzak Madjid the tabla; Kan'an Mohammed Saith and Dia Mahmoud Ahmed the deff. And the chanter, the poet? Yusuf Omar.

Yes, says Omar. This is your dream music. Listen again.

And Omar sings:

Oh these nights, these sleepless nights.
Who have I lost myself for?
A drunken man, a sober man, who have I lost myself for?
Take me to my home, take me to my home.
Who have I lost myself for
In these nights, these sleepless nights.

From the great tradition, he says. Or, one of the great traditions. In the dialect of my street, from a city far away. In fable, that is. But not so far across the black land.

19. The Venuses

I thought I was a scholar, I whisper to Omar. Until I met you. Sir, you understand everything on the island. Surely you can show me the gods. It's the gods I came for. Not the sailors. Not the fireflies. My research grant is spent.

Omar smiles.

I was at the bakery this morning, he says. Down the passageway I stepped and along that chancery. I saw a man carrying the hot trays, his mother counting the cents out on the mensa, flour in her eyes and apron. And the loaf she handed me? As big as an oxcart wheel. That's what I thought this morning. And I remembered wheels I once heard go rattling through the prickly pear. You will come with me.

And so the next evening I go to see the venuses. Omar directs me to the bus, but warns I will have to make my own way home.

It is the far side of the island. Wind blows, the stone dust flies. But the venuses are not hard to find. They sit together on a hillside looking east. The rain has worn their brows like temple steps. Loaflike they squat, and I think of Omar's loaf, his great wheel. For the venuses are loaf upon loaf. Their bellies are bread and their faces swollen dough, globular in the dusk and gilded with the last sun upon them. Sowlike I suppose, these beady-eyed matriarchs, with clefts in their bellies and shadows conglomerating in those gourds. A race of lumpen stone the venuses, looking where they have always looked. Forever out to sea.

I sit down. I sit amongst the Aphrodites in their ancient easiness.

How venerable these venuses. Their breasts and buttocks so cool under my fingers, these women who wait for time to stop, heads crushed into their shoulders' yoke, seven thousand years patient in this limestone sorority, their faces hidden, expressions concealed, knowing what they know and grown fat on the wind's salt, resting here on their millstones.

In the dark the gods are carboys of greenish wine. I gaze with them out to sea. The moon is coming up but is no whiter than their shepherd-polished thighs. These are the gods. These are the goddesses. They have survived so long that their religion is dead.

And I think of the women I passed on the track out of town, grandmothers come from market with halma and grapes. The last bus late.

Yusuf Omar (1918-1987) "was the last great traditional singer of the school of 'Iraqi maqams'."

The poem quoted occurs in the Baghdad sialect of Arabic and is an ancient popular lyrc, used in the 'Maqam Hsseini', "one of the seven fundamental maqams", and recorded for Ocora radio France, 1996, as 'Les Maqam de Baghdad'.

Cynffig

When the river reaches the sea it makes no fuss at all. There is no triumphal estuary, no saltmarsh or riverine flatland of grey glasswort. Simply a running over the cobbles and a low key disappearance. The landscape does not celebrate and the river refuses to exult. It is a small river with a corrupted name, a name older than the tree roots exposed in the dune walls, older even than its present course for this river has flowed several ways in its time.

Over the beach it runs, going quietly, its name the sound it used to make centuries ago, a gulp, a swallow, yet its consonants are still sharp against each other and a faultline divides its syllables. It is already a little brackish, poking its tongue into the ocean, a transfusion of warm effluent and acid snowmelt from the plantations on the hills behind.

When the twelve knights reached the river they stopped their journey. They decided there was a border that followed the river, up from the ocean and into the hills that gave little grazing and no grapes or honey, but sheltered a scattered people who chose to live in barren places. The knights built their fortress here close to the beach, and a town of a thousand souls grew about its walls, an important town that knew grapes and honey and poetry. Salmon were caught here, and trout whiskery as nettle flowers. Then the sand began to drift and the town was abandoned. The people moved away and history ceased. Sand was ruler now. It had settled in the wells and lapped the altar-stone. It smoked in the chancel and made minging rain. Out of the sea came the armies of sand, bloodying the air, their warcries of Chinese whispers. Yet the river still flowed and it remained a border. For the few travellers who came this way there was clearly a boundary here. The land changed; the air was different. When the travellers crossed the river they became different people.

Now I am neither one side of the border nor the other but amidst the border, the river on my skin, the water deeper, deeper as to be dangerous, befitting a border place. Fifty yards from shore the river is steeply banked and care is needed to withstand the wrestler, oiled and devious, that the current has become. The twelve knights could have grasped each others' arms and made a bridge across the water. The wrestler would not have troubled them. But they never crossed. They did not seek change or a country without grapes and honey. In the banks I see tree roots, gnarled as the river name, holding up the ramparts of sand and keeping everything together. And there is a stratum of plastics from BOC and ICI, and children's plastic toys and plastic shoes and ganglions of plasticated rope, as if possessions had been abandoned at the boundary, having no further relevance, such was the change that would occur after the crossing.

Change. That miracle. Destroyer of the inert. The American jet now overhead, the cormorant's skid from the skerry. All bringing change. The twelve knights understood it, their bones not much farther down than the Nike trainer and Datsun Sunny impacted in the bank, or the rhizomes of tetra-pak already under the surface of the sand. They were wary of these waters and stayed with what they understood. The river is slower now and more intricate. It is deeper than it looks. Beware, traveller, when you cross here, as one day you must. Glancing around you will see cranes against the sky, and venting flames, the iron dice of industry rolled upon the plain. When you breathe you will scent steel, acrid of late but sometimes delicate as the smell of cardamom and limes. Yes beware when you cross. There will be nothing to hold on to but yourself.

I'm Telling You Now

1.

The establishment is called 'Keats'. There's karaoke tonight and a slam next week. I order a JD and watch the bartender pour it to the tumbler brim. He gives me the once over but my hand's rocksteady.

And in that lunchtime bar I open the *New York Times* to learn that Freddie Garrity has died of emphysema. Another Sixties' relic killed by smoke. But sixty-nine's a long life in the music business. Not that Freddie was a star. On *Top of the Pops* he seemed a comedian, and in the US the biggest hit for Freddie and the Dreamers was that ludicrous shuffle, 'Do the Freddie'. I preferred 'You Were Made for Me', a Mancunian shanty you might imagine echoing round those redbrick Wilson's pubs with their brass nippled beer engines and typewriter tills.

Next I slip the stone out of my pocket. It's small and greyish red and fits my palm. One surface seems flat enough so I take the tweezers and scrape a letter. Then a second and soon I have my four letters cut. Holding it to my face I breathe in the stone's perfume. Then I unfold a sheet of paper. There are one hundred and thirty-six words on it. They include *ddodo* and *teli*. That'll fox 'em. The words make a poem about a time-travelling poet who died fifteen hundred years ago but is still flying around the world. At the moment he's in the Middle East. Yes, these are my materials: detonator and high explosive. See how the claquers like these babies. And I think, at the counter in Keats, the lunch-hour crowd starting to ebb, how easy it is to make a bomb.

2.

Moab might be Lot's grandson and massive ordnance air blast but tonight it's the mother of all burgers. Yet soon that neon charcuterie is left behind as we climb to Chapel Road and in the Datsun start to crawl round the hacienda.

Headlamps off, we're a black car in unpolluted darkness. The house too is unlit. The gates are closed and there's no guard.

But then, who is that? Up there in the tower? A figure is gazing, skywards of course, ever skyward, the telescope barrel pointing north east. So I look with it.

Hey, where did these come from? Such raw constellations: the Cactus, the Cadillac, the Tequila Worm. I've never seen them before.

Got to be Cage himself, hisses my companion. Built the house specially, didn't he? For the sky. The empty sky.

So while Nicolas Cage is scoping the sky we're stalking the stars. Yeah, Nick Cage. I think of him in *Leaving Las Vegas*, tipping that quart into himself like it was mother's milk. As if he was filled with ashes and he opened his mouth to a cloudburst. Call it irrigation. Then another Nick Cage in *8mm*, one man against the snuff-movie industry. On the side of life. The good guy.

Okay, maybe in reality he's not so great. Those sad tattoos? But you have to have a model, see. A role model. And Nicolas Cage is mine. Because Cage built an observatory. And now he's up there looking at all this; the fireflies, the UFOs, the shakedown of meteors over the desert. I can picture that glass he brandishes. Black lens with a rainwater meniscus set in a gold bezel.

So I'm here too, sneaking round his villa, me and the other obsessives in the pinon pine and prickly pear, all of us an audience outside his theatre. Because where else should we be, tell me that, when rising from the rimrock is this midnight moss of mescal-coloured stars?

3.

The stone comes from Cog y Brain. What's up there? A cool calcareous crater. A view of Gower and Cefn Bryn's brown volcanic cone. X-rays of coral. Buzzard bones like 64 ounce Big Gulp drinking straws. And from my botanist's roster, restharrow and bugloss, squill and squinancy. How did orchids, those stoics of limestone and loam, find their way? Why is centaury, the alchemists' herb, common this year? Below, every branch in Cwm y Gaer is a cambrel for cuckoo and crow. Ash keys shiver in their sheaves. A cock pheasant does the Freddie through the buckthorn. Not a bad place. Yet it will take me until the next millennium to understand it.

But scrape any rock on Cog y Brain. That's *brine*, and it was. The summit was once an ocean. This was the seafloor and its saltwater blood-warm. Tsunamis spun their camshafts here. Yes, select a stone and carve a word. Antediluvian viruses will be released, sulphur foam in the nose. The stones on that crest are brittle and fragrant. They snap like capsules and their dust floats away.

4.

Talking of role models, here's another. In the Guggenheim Museum's helter-skelter, it's the last day of the David Smith retrospective. Smith was a Brooklyn sculptor who taught, escaped teaching, worked like a foundryman to weld together his immense metal statements, drank too much and at 59 wrecked his car, cutting short a unique career.

In his steelies and leather apron, there's David Smith in the long grass of Bolton Landing. That's where he found sanctuary and inspiration. But a model? Undoubtedly. A big fisted shambling loner, Smith got on with the job. Sipping Jack Daniel's, brandishing his acetylene lance amongst a bushel of sparks, Smith dealt in wheels and axles and the dynamics of frozen motion.

In photographs he looks a bashful frontiersman. But that's what such people are. The USA is full of them. They make their art in the wilderness – in Gila Bend where it's hot as a griddle; amongst the redwoods in Santa Cruz; on the iron-angled sidewalk between Burritoville and the Café Vivaldi.

The caliphate that runs the Guggenheim has brought David Smith's art together. Here's the stuff that was weathering in the fields, all bloodrich iron, the portals and girders and gallows Smith set in his meadow.

But here too are his drawings. If Smith was a bison he's also a hummingbird. Every year he made four hundred large drawings. Let's forget talent for a moment. Industry, dedication, resolution are his other lessons.

But this might be his masterpiece. Here are David Smith's *Medals of Dishonor*, his predictions of the Second World War and what it would bring. The artist took a dentist's drill to incise bronze with some of the twentieth century's greatest war-warning art. His images are an indictment and iconisation of war and what creates warfare. Smith used horror derived from Hieronymus Bosch and satire from Brueghel the Younger to forge terrifying tableaux.

Looking at David Smith's work, displayed on every floor of the Museum Mile ziggurat, a ray passed through me. A dark laser. Maybe it had nothing to do with the exhibition. It concerned a human being's comprehension of how it must live, and then the struggle to fulfil that quest.

Not everyone rates David Smith. And maybe his art never made him happy. But there he is in dungarees that oxy's burned with its bulletholes. Dangerous stuff, oxy-acetylene. I worked with oxy once on the Cardiff foreshore when the scrappies from Bird Brothers were taking apart the hulk of *The Flying Fox*. The flame can droop loose and yellow. But at its hottest it's invisible.

5.

We go through the scanning process and file into the United Nations. With the other writers I put my stone on the auditorium stage. This rubble drawn from all over the world will be used in a 'poetry wall'. We were instructed to incise our language's word for 'poem' on our stones. As I know that English is not required, I have scratched a shaky GAIR. Which in Welsh means *word*. Because a stone isn't a poem. A stone is a word. So *gair* it is.

Then I read the poem I have selected. What can destroy might better delight, so nerve gas or nougat, bomb or bergamot, here are one hundred and thirty-six words about Taliesin, war poet who celebrated and surely detested war, who in these new words is stating fundamental truths. Which we will ignore.

When I cut the stone a prehistoric wind blew out of it. In Keats, I cupped its sulphur-smelling spore to my face. Like Monsieur Becquerel in his laboratory in Paris, Becquerel who had returned from holiday to discover radioactivity, I held the stone and let its demon enter where it would.

Freddie and the Dreamers Greatest Hits,(EMI) 1998.
'Taliesin' by Emyr Lewis, from Chwarae Mig (Barddas) 1995.
See www.davidsmiththeestate.org

The Reef

i.m. Joan Abse

But, Lord, thise grisly feendly rokkes blake,
That seemen rather a foul confusion
Of werk than any fair creacion
                                        The Franklin's Tale

In his fifties my father described himself as a beachcomber. I was puzzled by that until I reached the same age. Now I understand. My own writing is a beachcomber's diary whilst my editing work essentially beachcombing, with bottled messages of my own tossed into the electronic surf.

But literally (littorally?) I have become a beachcomber, discovering that the intertidal zone is the most dynamic part of the physical world I know, a world where I am closest to the processes that have fashioned this planet and the life upon it.

I'm in Southerndown on the coast of south Wales, where the sea snipes up the gwters to girn at the anglers on the bulwark and threaten night fishermen on Witch's Point. Twenty years ago I was employed here on the Glamorgan Heritage Coast as part of a Community Project *scheme*. I'll write that again – *scheme* – to bring back its unforgettable flavour. For *scheme* was a quintessential Thatcherite era word. And a bitter joke. (*Heritage* too is doublespeak. *Heritage* is the dirtiest deal we get).

But on the Heritage Coast I was the project manager. My colleagues were ex-soldiers and ex-prisoners, the workshy the feckless, the *didoreth*, the damaged, the dangerous, the doomed, the weird, the sick, the unlucky, the salt of the earth.

And I was one of them, paid the pittance that rescued the unemployed from moral corrosion and social uselessness.

In the summer of 1984 I had gained my Post Graduate Certificate in Education, yet had learned enough of comprehensives to know I would not become a teacher. (What an irony: since that decision I have visited more schools than a sales rep for Dorling Kindersley.) Instead, I was coasting.

Now at Southerndown I watch the sand migrate. It's a restless beast. What was hidden is revealed. But the familiar is lost. There's the barbarous ironwork of a buried deck, chain-link and hawser indistinguishable from the rim of a barnacled pool. And here, a two metre high honeycomb that marine worms have built over the rocks. Golden, oozing salt, it hisses electrically as the tide retreats. But out to sea a mile away is a white stave that becomes a black line. Something is emerging. Soon it is unignorable.

And I stare although I know what it is and have known all my life. It's an island, almost volcanic in the way it appears so abruptly, an island extruding into daylight and already clinkered with mussel shells, black with wrack. Rearing there is a reef like the roof of a submerged citadel. What's appearing is a mezzanine for conger eels, its razored edges sharp as conger teeth.

Once I stood here at a cave mouth. The waterfall that screens it was frozen into a glacier three yards wide, corrugated like a corkscrew. From within, or so it seemed, peered the faces of drowning children, blind eyed and hair afloat in that strange aquarium. Above, the cliff was snow-thatched, finials smoking in the breeze.

But this is a hot day in July. Around me lie boulders shifted from their prehistoric positions by the Bristol Channel tsunami of the seventeenth century. South and west are the emersable region and the splash zone where geology is speeded up and I might feel geomorphology happen between my toes. This is where avalanche and earthquake occur twice daily. Twice daily the littoral is constructed afresh.

This Glamorgan hides a life all right, cold blooded, hermaphrodite, cannibalistic. Rather seek mercy in the seawater-coloured eye of a passing gull than a rock pool's sumptuous mantling.

Yet I love these pools, especially after a storm when a black and green thallus floats upon every surface. For each pool is different. One's a dark jeroboam; one a saucer like a stoop in a church porch. One pool I know is a limestone cylinder, six feet deep, two feet in diameter, an immersion chamber wine-coloured with coralweed, its red becoming purple and its purple black, a cistern the sun will never irradiate yet which to me is a doorway to inestimable regions.

In my Heritage Coast year, Poetry Wales Press was based at Green Hollows Cottage, the home of Dannie and Joan Abse in Ogmore by Sea, half a mile away. For this reader at least, the books the press was then issuing remain central to my experience of those times. (Mass unemployment, the Miners' Strike, the core years of Mrs Thatcher). It was a wet summer in 1985. The schemies played cards in their hutch under the evergreen oaks. Heritage hung sodden around them.

I was thinking about that period on June 13th this year when Dannie and Joan Abse visited the Grand Pavilion in Porthcawl. They had planned a joint reading. Dannie had resigned from the Seren editorial board, a quarter century being enough committee work for anyone. For the event he chose poems of Ogmore and the Heritage Coast, fruitful and inexhaustible subjects.

As he and Joan read, I looked at the sea, visible through the Pavilion windows. It was the bluest it had been all year, the affirmative blue of a sea that is rarely blue. The tide was receding. And although it was concealed from view, something was thrusting from the waves.

Dannie Abse knew what it was. He read:

> ...*here, this mellow evening,*
> *on these high cliffs I look down*
> *to read the unrolling*

holy scrolls of the sea.

He read:

Has the past always a future?

He read:

> *The tide is out.*
> *And from the reeled-*
> *in sea – not from*
> *the human mind's vexed fathoms –*
> *the eternal, murderous,*
> *fanged Tusker Rock is revealed.*

And there lay that stark atoll. Which I observe now and to which I pledged particular regard when I worked on this beach for Mrs Thatcher's shilling. It will always be with us. Because in every summer sea as on every summer evening the reef must reveal itself.

Quotations from 'New Selected Poems' (Hutchinson, 2009) by Dannie Abse.

The Way They See It At Buba's

My brother, you know, is one of the conductors at the
Viennese opera.

Wonderful, I say.

Yes. For many years. We should toast him.

The barman pours us all a glass. One for himself, one for
me, and one for my new friend, the Slovene.

It is made of grass, says my friend.

I expect he means it's flavoured with herbs. A kind of
liquorice. Maybe aniseed. Because everywhere I go in this
country, the bottles are produced and the spirits, aromatic
and corrosive, are poured. Such rituals are vital. Local pride
is at stake. Usually, if you are drinking together it means you
are not fighting. So toasts are important.

Yes, says my friend, his dog curled at his feet. I can speak
English. And I can understand Croatian. But Croats have no
chance with Slovenian. No-one else here will understand us.
Now, what is it you are looking for?

The best way to arrive in Zagreb is by train. From the
west the railway follows the gorge of the Sava, the river
running green between limestone walls. But emerging from
the railway station I found that martial law prevailed. There
were police and soldiers everywhere. Roads were blocked,
entrance forbidden to state buildings, flights delayed. Of
course, a European Union delegation had arrived. This is
what always happens when such a delegation arrives in a
European capital. The city freezes like a computer. Our
leaders were in Zagreb to negotiate Croatian membership,
now a distinct possibility.

Obstacles to this are being overcome. Ante Gotovina's arrest late in 2005 at a Malaga restaurant and his speedy transportation to The Hague, where he will answer War Crimes Commission charges of ethnic cleansing and mass murder, has done a great deal to smooth the way for speedy admission. Many Western politicians view Croatian membership as crucial. Usually, the reasons given for this are bland, such as welcoming Croatia to the European family. Heard less frequently is the fear that fascism remains a latent political force in Croatia and that only EU membership will keep it reined in.

The Slovene stared at me hard. I could see he had decided to talk. And yes, he was correct. Of course I was looking for something. No-one visits Bistro Buba by mistake. Hidden away in its courtyard, Buba's is deliberately unprepossessing. I had come across the bar two years previously. Now, whenever I visit Zagreb, I find myself duty-bound to discover whether it's still there. But nothing seems to alter. The sink of unwashed crocks and the overflowing ashtrays are permanent fixtures. And in the gloom of the bistro, above the red and white check plastic tablecloths, the television will be on with a subtitled film.

British war films are popular in Croatia. I've seen Jack Hawkins ride *The Cruel Sea* in Buba's, the desert survivors wipe the froth from their lips in *Ice Cold in Alex*. Once there was a girl behind the counter, fineboned and palefaced, fragile in that proletarian twilight. She had opened my bottle of Karlovacko and smiled. But although I have looked, I have never glimpsed her again.

The Slovene shrugged. Bistro Buba, he said, is the last bar of its kind in central Zagreb. Everything around us changes. Everything costs more. Except here. Only Buba stays the same. I hope it always will.

For those who might wish to explore modern Croatian culture via the dangerous door marked *pivo*, this is a good place to start. Around the corner, The Old Pharmacy has opened, with its international lagers and perplexing English memorabilia. The Old Pharmacy is the new Europe, Buba and its Bubarians the unreconstructed continent. But my friend wanted to apologise.

Slovenia is already in the EU, he laughed. These Croats can't understand it. Maybe I can't. But the EU will want this country in sooner than later. Considering the past.

Then he told me what had occurred a few weeks previously. A crowd of thousands had gathered in Knin to mark the anniversary of the destruction of the breakaway Serb republic of Krajina in 1995. This had been set up in June 1991, the same time that Croatia and Slovenia formally declared independence from the Yugoslavian federation.

Croatia's 'Operation Storm', led by amongst others, General Ante Gotavina, had 'cleansed' Krajina, resulting in 300,000 refugees leaving the area. The tenth anniversary was marked by the Croatian Prime Minister, Ivo Sanadar, who described it as 'magnificent' and liberating. Many in the crowd had chanted anti-Roma slogans, for the gypsy situation in the new republics remains precarious. Then they had changed the cry to one of 'Ante, Ante', not only to mark General Gotavina's contribution, but as a tribute to the Second World War dictator, Ante Pavelic.

It is impossible to discuss Croatian fascism without reference to Ante Pavelic, premier of the 'independent state of Croatia' set up by the Nazis, 1941-45. Pavelic's territory consisted of two constituent parts – Croatia and Bosnia-Herzegovina, with a total population of 6.3 million. Of these, 3.3 million were Croats, almost all Catholic. There were 1.9 million Serbs, about 700,000 Muslims, 40,000 Jews and 30,000 Roma.

Although one of the great mass murderers of the Second World War, Ante Pavelic's name is hardly known in the UK. Yet he and his 'Ustasa' (Croatian Nazis) were responsible for the deaths of half a million Serbs and over one hundred thousand Jews and Gypsies. After the war, Pavelic was sheltered by the Vatican and employed by the Perons in Argentina. Indeed, Juan Peron issued over thirty thousand Argentine visas to Croats, not discriminating between pro-fascists and anti-communists, all of whom were fleeing Tito's post-1945 dictatorship. Eventually, Pavelic found a home in Franco's Spain, where he died in 1959.

Pavelic's plan was to exterminate a third of the Serbian population in Croatia, expel another third, and convert the remainder to Catholicism. Modern Croatian fascists, who feel their country's newly independent status is directly inspired by that wartime 'Independent State of Croatia' (Nazi puppet regime that it was) make a mystical relic of Pavelic's remains. His body is thought to rest at a secret location in Madrid. The return of the corpse of the 'Poglavnik' (supreme leader or Fuhrer) to Zagreb, with the possibility that Pavelic might lie there in state, is one of the great fascist dreams of Croatia.

Such mythification is in keeping with its powerfully dogmatic Catholicism that sets great stock on shrines and the bones of native saints. Indeed, the Croatian church, and especially the Franciscans, is inextricably linked with Croatian Nazidom. During the Ustasa reign of terror under Pavelic, many Serbs were forced to convert to Catholicism. These are deemed the lucky ones. If you know where to look, there are signs all over the country that Pavelik is still vener-ated by some Croats.

Of course, not all Croats were Fascists. Thousands joined Tito's partisans, while others were persecuted by Serbian Chetniks. It seemed that to oppose fascism, all non-fascists had to ally themselves with the communists, or in the south of Croatia, with the Serbian resistance.

But the crimes of the Ustasa tainted the nation. Thus during the Yugoslavian warfare of the early 1990s, it was normal for many Serbs to deem Croatia as 'fascist'. The Croatian leader and then President, Franjo Tudjman, was routinely blamed for rehabilitating the reputations and honouring the names of Ustasa members. He was also accused of trying to conceal evidence of the existence of the concentration camp at Jasenovac, set up by the Ustasa. This was in fact, a linkage of five individual camps located on the River Sava, sixty-five miles south of Zagreb. Estimates of numbers of Serbs, Jews, Roma, Muslims and non-Catholics murdered at Jasenovac range from 50,000 to nearly 100,000. Tudjman was also blamed by the Americans for airbrushing Croatia's World War Two record. For example, he changed the name of the 'Victims of Fascism Square' to 'the Square of the Great Croatian People'.

Franjo Tudjman, of the Croatian Democratic Union, was elected Croatian leader in the country's first ever free elections in April 1990. It took only eight months for a new Croatian constitution to be drafted, relegating the status of the 600,000 Serbs within Croatia to that of 'national minority' but without specified 'minority' rights. Thus the Serb state of 'Krajina' had been proclaimed. As I have noted, five years after the death of Tudjman, the current Croatian prime minister publicly gloated at its downfall.

When in Zagreb my first call is always the Dolac market. To make sure it is still there. This has almost become a duty. I knew I was late but some stalls were open. The familiar headscarved women were selling whey and cheese for frying; tables were spread with the yellow beans that I grow myself at home. But what was more important, the old woman was there in her usual position.

The last time I had seen her she was offering an apronful of chestnuts for sale. Today, it was rose hips. On her table were three branches of rose hips fatter than cherries. I drew closer. At least they looked like hips. But perhaps they were haws. Weren't haws a darker red? Maybe she had torn hawthorn twigs from a bush. No, they were hips, and I remembered at school splitting hips with my thumbnail to find the hairy seeds. Hips made itching powder to put down friends' backs. How we wriggled, the itchy eggs under our collars.

To the dog! ordered the Slovene.

Once again the barman filled our glasses with liquid from an unmarked bottle.

Never wake the dog, I suggested.

Oh no, he said. No, no. Unless you want it to bark. You see, the Croats have to be seen to be renouncing old ways. But it is hard. And it is very complicated. So it's best not to ask questions. Best never to ask.

I knew that soon after my departure, there would be an 'Anti-Fascism Day' proclaimed on November 9, the anniversary of 'Cristalnacht'. A great show would be made of erasing the graffiti endorsing Gotovina and Pavelic that disfigured public places. There would be many gatherings, including an anti-fascist rally at a mass grave in Kucibreg.

Before the Balkan war, Croatia's population was 12% Serb. Today that figure is less than 5%. Although there are new laws that stipulate refugee Serbs must be allowed to return to their original Croatian homes, they face major bureaucratic barriers. As do other minorities. For instance, Muslims today make up only slightly more than 1% of the population.

I never thought of Muslims until the war, says my friend at Buba's. I never met them in Slovenia.

What the Slovene means is the first Iraq War, and Operation Desert Storm. This televised conflict was dripfed into the bistro like everywhere else in the world.

But if anything changes this country it will be tourism. Croatia is now one of the world's most aggressively marketed tourist destinations. This is especially noticeable in the US, where the Adriatic regions are heavily promoted, and has the effect of confirming the region of Istria – long counter claimed as part of Italy – as integral to the Croatian state. At the same time, the sudden invasion of Italian, German and British second home owners is unwelcome to many Croats, as it pushes property values to heights considered absurd by locals. These days, tourism is responsible for over 15% of

Croatia's GDP, and the figure will grow.

I was relieved to see again the old woman of the Dolac. In reality, she is a peasant from the fields, bent and weather-beaten. But for me she is a Croatian symbol, and has stood in the market throughout her life, enduring dictatorship and war and the desperate jubilations of the Balkan crack-up. She knows the name of Pavelic, might have glimpsed him when a girl, and understands that some of her contemporaries still honour him. Tito she learned to love or loathe under her chestnut tree. Tudjman, Croatian leader after 1990, probably appealed. He possessed a sinisterly luminous political gift for conjuring national atavism.

Yes, there she stood in her corner of the square, and perhaps she will stand there to see Croatia become part of the European Union. I looked round the Dolac. All seemed well. They had packed up in the fish market next door and the sinks were being emptied. The Adriatic shoals with their Venetian names had vanished until tomorrow. A man was tipping ice out of a barrel and its smoke was rising, wraith-like, out of the drains.

Killing the Cool: The Outlook from Piemonte

We drive through a thunderstorm. The lightning hangs in ultra violet sheets above us. At times it seems to form enormous blue insect-o-cutors over the hills and vineyards.

Suddenly Alpine hail is gravel under our wheels and the Fiat is gusted across the road. But we arrive at the ristorante and the storm is refused entry. Now there is beneficence. A platter of truffles is paraded for our approval. Next, the Barbera and then the Barolo of Sandri Giovanni are poured in celebration. The toasts are emphatic. To poetry. To difference. To pride in tradition and what the imagination might do with it.

After the feast, the reckoning. Sometimes my tongue is a silversmith's hammer. The words are burnished beneath it. Yet too often, even I know, it is the mallet that perpetrates mayhem with the metrics of Twm Morys and mangles the muse of Mihangel Morgan. *Mimi, mae dy long wedi mynd,* I declaim. Yes, Mimi, you have missed the boat. A little later, Morys's last troubadour is laid apologetically to rest.

No matter. I am doing my best and detect no pain in the dark Piemontese eyes of the audience. The Welsh language has come in low over the Italian Alps and landed in bookshops and lecture rooms in Torino and Alba. As European languages go, it might sound unusual to the students, but it has clearly borrowed generously from Latin. Our words are a *pont* between us.

We're celebrating two new anthologies from Italy's

Mobydick press. Though they will not set the world alight, these are attractive volumes. But more than that, they are necessary books. It is crucial that Welsh writers escape Welshness. Being Welsh, after all, is an endless delirium. We rail at each other in the malarial earnestness of defining ourselves. But who cares? Certainly not those outside the fever hospital. It is time to emerge from our nightsweats. Some of the poets in these volumes show how it might be done.

Yet there are inherent dangers. If writing must be free-ranging it can also be well-rooted. Gerallt Lloyd Owen depicts the griefs of national conquest, but Emyr Lewis moves like mercury through the ancient metres, a surreptitious and slippery poet. For the English language writers, the dangers of cultural anonymity are greater. Amnesia International beckons. It's a seductive place to be.

Cultures often embrace each other in fear of a common enemy. In Piemonte, it was inevitably America, or rather the corporate USA that emerged as the threat. As a target it is irresistible. One way to encourage the students of the Langhe district to respond to our lectures was to predict that in one hundred years they will all be Americans. That Americanisation is a natural process to be welcomed. That in the next century we will construct ourselves with American-patented genes and cloned spare parts, as well as consume American food and art. That war and pestilence will be banished only when nations walk together under the golden clerestory of McDonald's.

You do not have to be a Piemontese or Ligurian speaker to blanch at this prospect. Across the Atlantic there are those who are equally aghast. For example, 'Adbusters' is an "ecological magazine, dedicated to examining the relationship between human beings and their physical and mental environments". Based in British Colombia, its audience is two thirds American. Adbusters further defines itself as "a global network of artists, writers, students, educators and entrepreneurs who want to launch the new social activist movement of the information age. Our goal is to galvanise resistance against those who would destroy the environment, pollute our minds and diminish our lives."

The enemies are those who purport to be *cool*. Who aspire to states of coolness. Who believe coolery has something to do with living to the max. Who think that coolism is to be embraced. Because to Adbusters, cool kills. Cool is a corpse in Rayban's. Cool stands for paralysis of the soul, the vanquishing of originality and variety. For Adbusters, cool is a totalitarian world built to a consumerist blueprint. It is policed by style fear. Cool is paranoia. As a formula, cool = orthodoxy. And for the artist, cool = death.

To make war on cool, Adbusters employs the weapons of cool – the iconography of adverts and rock music. It has created 'powershift' – an advocacy advertising agency that uses the global language of entertainment and brand names to subvert what it sees as the corporate hex big business has placed on our world.

Rock is especially important. Modern music (the wisdom goes) used to be challenging and thrilling. Once it demonstrated how writers and musicians could enrich traditional forms with new energies and ideas. Today rock is a global neurasthenic plague. Yet if it sounds like the bleating of babyminds, it is really brilliantly orchestrated money-music. The planet wears headphones and our fate is to listen to a digitalised hymn to corporate greed. Rock music, say the Adbusters, is nothing but the amplified death rattle of our own imaginations.

If so, Little Richard, strutting down his piano keyboard in 1955, has a lot to answer for. Yet inevitably, there are rubies in the rubble. The group, Catatonia, wrote an ironic song that runs 'Every Day When I Wake Up I Thank the Lord I'm Welsh', covered by Tom Jones. Unfortunately coolness and irony cannot cohabit. The latter devours the former. So the song was taken literally by the Welsh media as evidence of

Wales being somehow fashionable. It did not occur to the newshounds that the only cry of the artist can be: 'every day when I wake up I thank the Lord I'm human.' Or at least, sober. Or if you're Tom Jones, rich. Or if you're Little Richard, making a comeback.

One of the editors of Adbusters is Kalle Lasn, who published *Culture Jam: The Uncooling of America*, (Eagle Brook, $25). Lasn believes the only way we can create a tolerable future is by uncooling ourselves, i.e. by celebrating human cultural and imaginational diversity, instead of representing them as barriers to profit and the growth of the corporations. Maybe the crucial question Lasn asks in *Culture Jam* is 'what does it mean when a whole culture dreams the same dream?' History, of course, provides the terrifying answers.

Writers and readers might be puzzled here. Surely, the route to discover the real America is via its art. From Dickinson to Lowell, from *Moby Dick* to the poetry of Cormac McCarthy's novels, that is where America might live for us. Or we can listen to Mississippi and Chicago blues, attend the platforms of Latino poets, pray in a sweatlodge. We can learn about America through its environment, watching geese skidding down on frozen Massachusetts wetlands, or shielding our eyes from the dazzling porcelain of a Californian drybed. That is surely the way for the individual.

Yet America does not communicate itself like that to the world. Rather America speaks thus: "...if we make it impossible for... people to escape Coca Cola...then we are sure of our success for many years to come. Doing anything else is not an option". (*Coca Cola Annual Report*).

And "...we'll someday sell a variety of products on a daily basis to every living person on the Earth". (*Pepsico Annual Report*).

And "We are moving across the oceans and into new states and blocs. The joy of it is there is no speed limit to our progress... Rather, the cheering will grow louder and stronger the faster we go...especially from our share-owners". (*Campbell's Soup Company Annual Report*).

To these, now add the pronouncements of gene-splicing and biotech companies. This is the America that Kalle Lasn targets, using its own armaments of 'mind bombs' and 'meme warfare'. To make a mind bomb, Adbusters takes an advert like "escape to Calvin Klein" and prints picture and text as normal. Except 'to' is changed into 'from'. Seen on the page, so inured are we to the original, nothing looks different. But an explosion, Lasn would insist, has occurred in our subconscious.

Maybe. But once again I suggest it is easier to turn to American literature, which offers online guerrillas all the weaponry of revolutionary thought and mind piercing literary ammo they can use. In this respect, a page of Melville or Lowell is nitro-glycerine. If, as a culture, we read more, and remembered our reading, we would know this instinctively. Because books are our allies and will always be there. Our peril is that we will forget how to read them.

On the day we arrived in Piemonte, McDonald's announced plans to double the number of its Italian outlets. From what I saw, this would make little impact on a region confident of the validity of its traditions, the future of its culture. If the young love the burger chain, most older people find it as attractive as the Albanian mafia. In Diano d'Alba, there was room only for hearty appetites. A vintage Barolo was being broached in happy conjunction with the book launches. (For tipplers, this wine is a snorting indigo beast, sacrificially garlanded with sorrel and Alpine gentians.) It washed down beef, wild boar, rabbit, and raw Langhe veal minced fine as a spider's web. Big Macs and the emaciated imagination and oedematous ambition that have created them, were not conspicuous.

Yet the future, of course, will not be literary. It belongs to film, although assembling a novel is as thrilling and demanding work as any now experienced by young people switching on the power of their personal editing suites.

And I look forward to a society where science receives its due. Where workshops in physics, astronomy and yes, biotechnology are as common as writing classes today.

The Dictatorship

I step off the path. And into the woods. How easy to get lost here. The air is full of resin whose grandmotherly jewellery, cairngorms and zircons, is strung around the pines.

But what are these? Loaves dipped in red wine, nuns in black who have painted their faces gold. Here is the death cap in its clergyman's collar, the fly agaric's acne on a rosy cheek. Fallen under the birch are the dead with holes in their heads.

At the sides of the road wait the mushroom sellers. It is autumn and the forests are full of fungi. A woman has laid a napkin on the grass, the entrepreneurial young erected stall and awning.

The roads run straight between the trees, and although there is no traffic yet, the mushroom sellers offer their harvest, reputed to be excellent. Our van turns down a track into a car park.

We're five miles outside the Lithuanian town of Druskininkai on the border with Belarus. At the museum entrance is a soviet evocation of 'Spring', enormous yet not without grace. Spring too could be put to work, its rite propagandised and suborned. And yet this maiden with arching limbs, giantess in her joy, has a poignancy now.

Such museum parks are found throughout what was the 'Eastern bloc'. True, these are tourist sites, but for me they are amongst the most important places in our new Europe.

I wander off to meet the dictators. There is Lenin, there Stalin in his worker's weeds; and here the ferro-concrete images of the forever shamed, carried from squares in Vilnius and Kaunus, the collaborators, the placemen, the true believers. But here is Hitler too, and the henchmen of the Third Reich. Pogrom, purge, purgatory, this is Lithuania during its double occupation and desperate decades.

The faces of the disappeared stare from the walls of the galleries. Martial music plays from loudspeakers in the trees. There are recreations of peasants' huts and the shelters of those who hid, hid for years in these forests, writers amongst them.

Everything takes place in the woods – glade after silent glade of birch and pine. I walk with the Estonian poet, Jaan Malin, in the cemetery. Graves have been dug between the trunks, not trees planted between graves. We kick through the upholstery of needles, scaring red squirrels. Druskininkai is a quiet place. Its citizens wander past under the leaves. They seem preoccupied.

Strangely, I think about rubbish. At home, anything we throw away is taken to an incinerator. There, all recyclables are salvaged by hand. The people who do this are Lithuanians. In Porthcawl library they book time on the internet.

Labbas ritas I said to one woman. She looked away as if I could read her thoughts. Or as if she had read mine from the contents of my dustbin. Clever, determined, such people are welcome in democratically-fatigued Wales.

That woman is a harbinger, I have no doubt. Since 2004, Lithuania has been a full member of the European Union, and change in that country, as in all the former Soviet occupied states, is astounding.

Traffic, at least in the towns, grows exponentially. New banks ring the squares, and in Vilnius, a once dangerous district such as Uzupis with its anarchist and gypsy history, offers apartments for wealthy incomers. This is a Europe of incessant movement, where the ambitions of the formerly oppressed are palpable. But what flux. The young and energetic coming one way, the middle aged with their appetites for sun, self-expression and *meaning* going another.

It seems a fair exchange. Yet there is people-smuggling also, and a vicious sex trade. Lithuanian odalisques, lupin-eyed, spruce-white laths, are part of its currency.

Yes, the mushroom harvest is good this year. Some of these forest steaks are thick as EU environmental edicts. But, my companions have warned, we dare not eat the mushrooms. Look at the map. The mushrooms carry the poisons of an old Europe, the wisp of Chernobyl that endures more powerfully here than almost anywhere else, a dictatorship that will survive for three billion years, and on every June 26, celebrates its anniversary.

Salvaging the City

The gates were open but there was no-one about. I spent an hour in the yard looking at the roofs that had been dismantled over the last decade, the bricks and lintels, newel posts and railings.

Here was the capital of Wales laid low, Cardiff stacked in wire cages: doorknobs, chimneys like pantomime crowns, all boxed into the Lego of an Alzheimic language that would never be spoken again.

In the warehouse I went upstairs. There was a black school honour board against the wall. In gold letters was my uncle's name: 1933, a silver medal. And again 1933, a scholarship of £100 to Jesus College, Oxford. Ivor Minhinnick died young, but not before he had written a mathematics text-book once in regular use. Maybe the book was here too, with the *Hymnau Calfinaidd* and Showaddywaddy albums.

It took time to find my bearings. There's a new route system in this part of the capital, but eventually I stepped back on to the beach. I hadn't been there for years and the views have changed.

Yet the beach was the same. Like a shelf in the salvage yard, all swarf and glowering agglomerations, steelworks sinter and the taste of rust sharper than seasalt. For rust is Tremorfa pollen, the rust from the wreckage at Bird Brothers, that emporium of rust where I tallied what we tipped the tattermen for their scrap cars, checking the comptometer print-out and filing the dockets on a spike. I was back at the beach, on Cardiff's cankerous brink. It crumbled underfoot like wirewool. The darkness seeped in.

A mile west but in another dimension is 'Cardiff Bay'. The Wales Millennium Centre was a beacon in the rain. For someone like me who opposed the building of the Cardiff Barrage and sentimentalises the lost Hogarthian tableaux of the Mount Stuart Hotel, it's a welcome sight in a capital of overpriced apartments and theme-bars. Gwyneth Lewis was commissioned to write two verses integral to the Centre design. Now her poetry shone enormously into the night. Upstairs I stood behind the words and each was a lens of a lighthouse: *awen horizons ffwrnais stones*. And *gwir*, a difficult word to understand, especially when it's a sequin sewn into the Cardiff skyline. But there it is. An honour board that cannot be taken down. Lewis's most momentous publication.

How badly needed it is in a development described as 'the most exciting waterfront in Europe'. Soon it will illuminate Wales's first dedicated parliamentary building for seven hundred years, a political aquarium for the poor dabs who rule us and a glass tank in which the aspirations of the country will be revealed.

Mark Jenkins's monologue, 'Playing Burton', was running as the Millennium Centre's first studio play. It has the elements of real tragedy. With two hundred others I listened to a man the spit of Richard Burton but who lacked the sinew of his voice. No matter. I shut my eyes and remembered an actor aspiring to academia, a lion bored with the pride.

Burton spoke two endangered languages: Afan Valley Welsh and Marlovian English. We learned about his retinue: Dic Bach, Philip the svengali, Elizabeth Taylor.

And about vodka which by the end literally inhabited him. In hospital for an operation, surgeons had to scrape crystallised alcohol from his backbone. But the play's eighty minutes never contained a silence. Not once was Burton simply *there*. Not a facial muscle or gesture indicated his incredulous despair. He was swaddled in words like mummy-cloths.

At Bird Brothers, the tattermen were usually Irish gypsies.

They would park twice on the weighbridge while I subtracted. Around us the drams dragged past and the shears hung in silhouette over my hutch. Cardiff was khaki then, the morfa of Tremorfa ashen as Saskatchewan.

Now Birds' is a way of life. For those who can interpret such things, its gantry lights spell their own poems. Two million new cars are bought each year in the UK. The oxides await.

That day on the shore I had let my feet read the scrappies' industrial braille. From there you can see the city going up like a field of mushrooms. And even if it appears an environmentalist's apostasy, I say let it prosper. Let all its poetry burn.

What They Take

I think I was eight. The man said turn over and lie on your tummy. So I did. He rubbed his wet finger along my spine as if he was looking for something.

Then he said this might hurt. I wondered why he would want to hurt me. And anyway, I'd gone sort of numb.

You're brave, aren't you? he asked. I've heard you're very brave.

The man said don't look. So I stared at the pillow which was thin and striped. A hard pillow, harder than at home. But out of the corner of my eye I'd already seen what he was holding. I must have cried. And I could feel his hand on the small of my back.

How cold I must have seemed to him. A boy of eight, white as a wood shaving. And skinny, because I was skinny then. My ribs showed, my back was no wider than a white line in the road. I must have looked like a wishbone on that bed. Yes, legs spread, arms outstretched. And me white as a wishbone.

No, the man said. And he laughed. You don't lie flat. You must be a squirrel. You're a squirrel with your tail in the air. With your chin on your chest and your paws in front.

So I became a squirrel. How horrible it was, I thought, to be a squirrel. How wrong it felt. But I could see what he was going to do. It was big as a bicycle pump, that hypodermic and I might have cried. Or whimpered, because that's the proper word. Isn't it?

Don't look round, he said. And stay very still. You don't move a muscle. All you have to do is count. Be brave now and count. So I counted.

No, he said. Count slower. And don't move. So I counted more slowly. More slowly like this.

Oooone.

Twooo.

Threeee.

Like that. And his hand was as wide as my back and the needle went into my skin between his fingers. I imagine that's the way he did it because that's the way I would have done it. And then the needle went into the bone.

When I think about it now what I see is an aspen leaf. The underside of a leaf with the veins showing. A pale leaf. Because that was me. I was a squirrel no more, I was light as a leaf. So light I might float away if his hand didn't hold me down. Didn't press me down into that starched sheet. My face above the striped pillow. Which was wet, I can feel it now. Wet somehow.

I had counted so long I couldn't believe it. There was no such number as eleven. When I had reached ten I thought he would be finished. Ten was the number I had been aiming for. And when I stopped he said count, keep counting. And keep still.

You see, he said, this isn't your medicine. I'm not putting medicine into you. No. I'm taking something out. Of you. Something very precious. Away. I haven't found it yet. But when I find it I'll take a little of it and then we'll test it and that will tell us everything. Tell us what is giving you these dreams. And then we'll know how to stop them.

Because I was ill, I knew that. I was ill with dreams. At home my mother had placed her hand on my forehead, her nurse's hand, and she knew I was dreaming. And my father sat me down in the rocking chair and he asked "Do you see the animals? Do you see the animals?"

We had all been out for a walk. We were in the aspen wood. When I walked into the wood I was myself. Unchanged. When I came out of the wood I could feel the sunlight turning to ashes in my head. I felt stiff. There was a steel reinforcing rod pushing up through my spine. One of those rusty rods you see in concrete.

And yes, I could see the animals. I could see the weasel with his magician's white gloves. And I could see the viper, and its hollow tooth. The tooth full of delirium.

The needle was in me still. I could feel it between those blue stones of my back. That was why they had brought me to the fever hospital. Because I came out of the wood with my head on fire they brought me to the fever hospital and put me behind the glass. Where I sat and watched every day as the cars arrived and the mothers delivered their children wrapped in linen, holding them to their breasts. Holding their children like the long stems of roses, the thorns clinging a moment to their sleeves.

That's it, said the man. And I could feel the needle slide out of me and I imagined it as an icicle because what else could a boy of eight imagine, the steel of that needle so thin it was invisible.

Here it is, he said. No, don't move. And he came from behind me to show the hypodermic and in the hypodermic was a golden liquid.

Yes, it had come out of my body. Out of my spine. What a colour it was. Oh yes, it was molten gold. I was rich.

From your nervous system, he said. A dangerous place. A very dangerous place to meddle with. But needs must.

I remember that phrase. Needs must. And there was the golden water. There was the molten gold and I was still crying and maybe I was still counting, still counting, one million and twelve, one million and thirteen... But I was proud. I know I was proud.

Because that golden water made me who I was. And I thought, yes, like Jason and the Argonauts. I'd seen the film in the old Palace, which is pulled down now. And nothing was ever built where the Palace stood. They could never replace the Palace.

The argonauts met a giant on an island. An iron giant.

And the only way to beat the giant was to open the valve on the giant's heel so that his golden water ran away, ran steaming and fizzing into the sand, the giant growing weaker and desperate, the elixir pouring out of him, that smoking jism, until he crashed down.

The giant was dead, I suppose. And ever since, I've had that fear. It's inevitable that I've had that fear. That the water in me, my elixir, will drain away. Through my skin. Through a cut. That I might piss it away, that golden water, wherever it comes from. By mistake. Somehow purge myself of that golden water. Expel myself from myself. The best part of myself. The real part.

No, he said. No, don't move. We don't want to do this again, do we? We don't want to take too much. And then he was gone and the nurse allowed me to lie on my side and she pulled the sheet over me, and she whispered into my ear.

But I could still feel the man's hand on my back. Could still imagine I might float away. I was a leaf, you see. An aspen leaf.

Such a tree, the aspen. You must have seen aspens. They sigh in the wind, they never stop moving. Swaying and sighing, that's aspens. Like that man, standing over me. Like the nurse. What did she say?

But there are some people who call aspen trees girls' tongues. Yes, girls' tongues. And other people who call aspens old women's tongues. Is that because aspens sigh? Or because aspens are never still?

Because aspens are not pieces of wood. When I see aspens I see the sap inside them. A circulation of sap that doesn't stop. Because to me aspens are like fireworks that never burn out. Their sap never dries up. You know, they crucified Christ on an aspen tree. And gave him vinegar to drink.

And I could feel the nurse's breath on my neck. I could feel her girl's tongue, or was it her old woman's tongue, and her hand now in that cold place of my back. I could hear her saying something.

Then I must have fallen asleep. Or should I say I must

have woken up. Anyway, I exchanged one dream for another. Because the bed was moving around on its wheels. And the nurse was pushing the bed, pushing it through the stream where I played, catching gwrachens with my hands, pushing it through that fierce stream until we reached the sea. And then the ocean. She was pushing me through the ocean and whispering to me.

But even as I slept I was awake. And I knew that somewhere in the fever hospital, the man was walking down a corridor and the sun was shining through the windows and bathing him in light. He was carrying a bottle and in that bottle was a teaspoon full of golden soup.

And the man would pause and hold up the bottle to the light to look at what he had stolen from me. Because I know now what it was. There's no doubt about it. He had stolen a drop of my soul.

Scavenger

1.

A night of fat stars.
The sky full of blister packs.

2.

Just like the sea. There are times when the sea's as clean as I can remember. Others when it tries to spew everything out of itself. I could build a city from the plastic I kick through at the caves. A million sandwiches still in their packaging. Thousands of planks, six months, twenty years in the water, and yet I smell the forest. Those jewels of resin.

3.

Zigmas drowned. That's what they said. Even before the deluge and the biggest waves. He could have escaped like the rest but he ran to the ghost train and hid in a carriage on the rail. In the dark.

He was one of the Lits, we all knew, from somewhere in the south of that country. Not the Baltic, where people would have understood the ocean.

Someone said Zigmas had never seen the sea before he arrived at the fairground. He told people his father was a mushroom seller. It seems he thought he might have been safe. But in the ghost train? What can you say about people like that? There was also a girl drowned in the subway, under the school mural. You know, I think they get what they deserve. Why should I worry about those simple kids?

4.

Breathing. That's what I can hear. The stone, breathing. It's what I've always heard in Pink Bay. No, not the sea sighing, because sometimes the tide is far away. But in this place, where the limestone meets the sandstone, the red bleeds into the grey, I can hear the stone itself. Its ancient exhalation.

I didn't think like that as a child. It's something I've gradually learned I'm able to do. If I pay enough attention. Because that's something I'm good at. Paying attention. Yes, if I listen long enough I hear the sound of stone breathing.

But there are so many voices we never hear. Because we've forgotten how to listen. I mean really listen. Which is what I do when I come here.

Never alone now, are we? I mean, properly alone. That's vanished. Think about most people. They have no idea what it's like to be solitary. Or singular, a better word. What singularity can mean. Another reason to pity them.

5.

We used to bring cheese and bread. Packets of chocolate biscuits with milk for the morning. And booze, of course, that was the point. Dregs of sloe gin, the peppermint schnapps nobody ever drank, advocaat, grenadine. Anything we could filch unnoticed.

How bright those bottles were, our terrible cocktail. When I think of it now, they were the colours in the cave itself, yellows and purples, like bruised flesh. And the stone too, how alike it is to the human body, voluptuous and intricate.

In the candlelight we sang and played guitars, and I'd find my fingers straying to the stone. I'd stroke the stone as if it was alive. No matter the weather, that rock was always wet. And fissured like flesh, I discovered. Yes, one of my great discoveries.

6.

I think I've slept. I know I lay down and tried to make myself comfortable. The sandstone is hard. I had a sleeping bag with a blanket but it is so humid now I didn't need it. The weather again is strange. But the weather's always strange. These days. Neither was I sure of the tide, because the ocean doesn't behave as you think it should. As the sea once did. But I know I lay down and thought. And dreamed a shark in the fairground. The mall was flooded, and someone said the types of tides we have today have not been seen since Neolithic times. No, millions of years, they said. It was a voice in my head said that. Someone whispering to me. A lover, almost. Another of my voices. There are so many.

The shark was lost, misplaced from the deeps. Yet a shark still, a shark bewildered, that shark a victim too, but a shark all the same, a grey glimpse, a shadow that shark, out of the dark shoals, a shape in the ruins with all the storm debris, the archipelagos of shit, the new atolls. A shark in the shallows.

So I shivered into and then out of sleep.

When I woke for the last time I tried to open my eyes. But all I could make out was the blood colour of my own eyelids. Exactly what you see when you gaze into the sun. The red colour of sea anemones. Their raw flesh on the rock, shivering to the touch, like wet flowers. And I rubbed my eyes but the red colour remained the same. So I squeezed my eyes and licked my lips, tasting last night's supper, the wine crust around my lips, a ring of salt. Fierce that salt, its burn, its sting.

And a taste too of Lizzy's mouth where she had kissed me that time long ago, Lizzy's own wine-tasting tongue, the tang of her own salt, because all of us must taste the same now, wherever we are, though it's hard to think many remain. I'd say we taste of salt and sand and cheap whisky, of the smoke we suck into ourselves. Yes, we taste of the sunblock we have to use, even when it rains. We taste of sweat, dirty-sweet, as we tasted of the smoke from our driftwood fire that night, the wrack burning green as iodine. That time we lit the fire. The time Lizzy kissed me.

Once we tasted of the seawater that poured through the kitchen of the Blue Dolphin café. When the drains ruptured and the tide was huge. There used to be a picture of a shark on the wall there. Maybe that's why I dreamed about the shark. No, there was no photo of a dolphin. And I tell you, it was real, that flood. Real in my dream. The arcades, the rides, all of it was underwater, and the shark grey in the black waters between the carousel horses and the characters from Star Trek, the horses with their names, Madeline and Myfanwy, painted on the golden poles. Someone said they were still going round, as the different currents pushed them one way and then pushed the other. Think of those dead children. Going round on the carousel.

And those Star Trek heroes? Each was drowned and swollen in the swell. I watched as the bears from the shies washed past, ruined of course, the pandas and koalas, the stuffing oozing out of the bad stitching. What they sold on those stalls was the cheapest gear possible. Sewn by slaves in Vietnam and Bangla Desh. But imagine everything ruined and everything spoiled. All those prizes.

7.

I had expected the tide to wake me and was ready for that. But I was ahead of myself. Instead I awake to a crimson world, the sandstone redder than any stone I've ever seen, the sky pink, yes pink as that flower that grows in the dunes. Soapwort they call it. People long ago used to boil the roots to wash their clothes. I tell you, it's well known. That pink flower, almost as tall as a man. Or maybe its seeds, I can't remember, perhaps they boiled the seeds for soap. I'm still thinking about the shark, but finally my eyes are open. As I lie here astonished. By this crimson world.

Molten, this world. And I think, yes, I know this world. As it had been when it first formed. Volcanoes, their rivers of lava like the planet's blood.

This new world is where I lie and have awoken. The shape of the shark is still dark in my dream and the prize bears are floating on the tide, and everywhere the smell of rot. Deep down, the stink of rottenness. And a child's shoe floating by.

8.

I lie where we always walked. It was a place famous amongst us. Others loved it, yes, generations had walked here, had been drawn to the red beach. There are patterns of white quartz that children always said was writing. I'd thought and said the same myself when I was young, when I looked at the quartz in the rock, a white language in the red sandstone, and tried to make sense of those hieroglyphics. As if it was an explanation. Yes, when I was eighteen I was certain the quartz said and meant something. If only I could decipher it. Which would be the challenge of a lifetime. And become my great work.

I've slept here once before, when I lay tracing with a wet forefinger the secret language. Who's to say it wasn't a warning? Who can be sure we haven't already been told what will happen? The white lettering, gleaming, like crystal milk, ignored all this time. And now it's too late.

That was the first flood. 'The inundation' they called it on the news. These days the waves are higher and come further in. But the fairground reopened, as it always does. And the Blue Dolphin started up again, selling its cheap food. That food people around here were brought up to eat, the chips, the faggots and peas. Twice to my knowledge it's been flooded out, and twice tried again.

When Zigmas died many other people drowned, but I remember only Zigmas. That strawberry birthmark on his cheek, his hair so blonde it was almost white. Yes, it's only Zig I dream about, a boy running into the ghost train tunnel, thinking he'd be safe. People say the water rose to the roof, the hounds of hell floated away when their chains came loose.

The hounds' eyes were yellow as the quartz in the cave.

Most days now I'm out on the peninsula. Yes, the tides can be huge, but when the water's low I explore the caves. Chilly places, even when it's hot. And dark as dungeons. Once I found a drowned porpoise, its beak a mattock of polished bone. But when the sun is in the right place the light shines directly into the cavemouths. That's when you see the starfish, the anemones. Violet and red, those creatures. I listen to their breathing, the music they make.

Yes, since the inundation I've been relearning the old skills. Teaching myself what we should never have allowed ourselves to forget. That's the reason I've decided to live here. Because my father told me he was a beachcomber. Or that's what he said I'd become. Yes, he used to say, all of us will be beachcombers, one day. Almost a prophet, I might say. That was my father. And I am his prophecy.

But there's no food here. And all the world tastes of salt. The caves so smooth, so cold, taste of salt when I lick the crevices in the limestone. The rocks, the starfish, they all taste of salt. Have you ever eaten starfish? Or sea anemones? Boiled or fried I can't make them taste of anything but salt. Even with a samphire garnish, a side of coralweed.

So we're all scavengers. Yes, that's what they call me but that's merely another word for beachcomber. And if you know your history you'll be aware how people around here lived. They took whatever washed ashore, the brandies, the silks. Everything a staved hold supplied. They were wreckers, I suppose. Old skills passed down the generations. How often was the riot act read to clear the beaches of men days drunk? In World War Two a cargo of Guinness was lost and divvied up. And there is so much else afloat these days. The ocean's become a rubbish tip, burning, steaming. Yet still it teems with bizarre creatures. That shark gives me nightmares, but there are sunfish now, swollen like zeppelins. *Mola mola* they call the sunfish, fat and round and silver with blue tattoos. More like the moon.

I look at the moon from the cavemouth where I camp, sometimes from the red container where the lifeguards kept their gear. All those surfboards and paddles? I burned them on the beach. There are so many camps now in the dunes, or out on the sand, it takes time to learn the protocols of fire.

Last year I came upon a sunfish of monstrous size. Over a ton, it surely was, and stranded on rocks. When ripped open, its belly was full of plastic bags. I dined for three weeks off the creature, as long as I dared. Salty steaks, but that's how the world tastes now. I had to use my stick against the dogs. These days I carry a piece of lead piping. Perfect heft in my hand, that bludgeon. But there are so many dogs now. Even in the caves I hear them baying at night. Those Alsatians look and sound like wolves. Big as the hounds of hell. Of course I need a weapon.

Nights, I'm sometimes in the cave. The same place Lizzy kissed me, though maybe, look, maybe it was mutual. Or maybe I might have touched. Her. On the breast, perhaps. That's natural isn't it? No reason to run away. Was there? But it's a different world now. I don't have time to worry about that. The old laws don't apply.

9.

Zigmas loved the forest. The sawn wood that washed ashore? Those thousands of white staves? It might have been his home over there in Litland. He came to the fairground, beside a foreign sea, to a place where no trees grew and only salt thrived. A world of caves and a prophesy in quartz. Somewhere he could have never imagined. The frayed edge of a continent. Where the land is drowning.

Now look, twenty miles across the bay is the Meridian tower. A splinter, the colour of cuttlebone, built for those who thought they owned all they surveyed. I've been there once, a week's expedition. The dogs are bad but people are worse. There are places where the land's officially abandoned, but I ignore all that. I picked a way through the rubbish brought ashore by the new tides. Such adventures I've had. The faces of the drowned...

But I can't get Zigmas out of my mind. That's why I dream about him, he's one of my ghosts, a boy brought up in an ocean of trees who had never seen a beach. They said he couldn't swim for that reason, and I see the filthy water rising in the tunnel, Zigmas in the dark with all the glass cases smashing as they topple about him, the flood reaching his chin, his eyes. Zigmas in the tunnel with the worst things in the world...

10.

The stars have vanished. As they do. I'm awake now on a painted beach. Yes, the stone is breathing. I know the stone is alive. Under my body what's written in quartz spells out this world's fate. I feel the letters burning into my skin. Yes, it's agony, but I will lie here as they brand me, those words, and one day people will come to read the living prophesy.

I used to look at the sky and the jet trails there. I thought that was writing and it was written for me. The white lines were like quartz in the sky. But I was wrong. The prophecies have been here all along, given to me alone to understand. When I move I will be ready. And I am almost ready....

Acknowledgements

Versions of some of the writings in *Island of Lightning* have previously appeared in *Poetry Wales, Planet, New Welsh Review, Lampeter Review, I Know Another Way* (Gomer), and the play *A Few Little Drops* (Volcano)

SEREN

Well chosen words

Seren is an independent publisher with a wide-ranging list which includes poetry, fiction, biography, art, translation, criticism and hstory. many of our authors have been on longlists and shortlists – and have won – major literary prizes. among them the Costa Award, the Man Booker, the Desmond Elliott Prize, the Ondaatje Prize, the Writers' Guild Award, the Forward Prize and the T.S. Eliot Prize.

At the heart of our list is a good story told well or an idea or history presented interestingy or provocatively. We're international in authorship and readership though our roots are here in Wales (Seren means Star in Welsh), where we prove that writers from a small country with an intricate culture have a worldwide relevance.

Our aim is to publish work of the highest literary and artistic merit that also succeeds commercially in a competitive, fast-changing environmet. You can help us achieve this goal by reading more of our books – available from all good bookshops and increasingly as e-books. You can also buy them at a 20% discount from our website, and get updates about forthcoming titles, readings, launches and other news about Seren and the authors we publish.

www.serenbooks.com